The Living and Active Word

THE LIVING AND ACTIVE WORD

One Way to Preach from the Bible Today

by O. C. EDWARDS, Jr.

A CROSSROAD BOOK
The Seabury Press · New York

The Seabury Press
815 Second Avenue
New York, N.Y. 10017

Designed by Paula Wiener
Printed in the United States of America

LIBRARY OF CONGRESS CATALOGING IN PUBLICATION DATA

Edwards, Otis Carl, 1928–
    The living and active word.

    "A Crossroad book."
    Bibliography: p. 173
    1. Bible—Homiletical use. 2. Preaching. 3. Protestant Episcopal Church in the U. S. A.—Sermons. 4. Sermons, American. I. Title.
BS534.5.E38   251'.08   74-30038
ISBN 0-8164-0265-5

The word of God is living and active, sharper than any two-edged sword, piercing to the division of soul and spirit, of joints and marrow, and discerning the thoughts and intentions of the heart.

HEBREWS 4:12

To My Parents
Who gave me ample opportunity to
cut my teeth on the back rail of a pew

Acknowledgments

Both the method advocated here and the examples to illustrate it grew out of three years spent at Trinity Episcopal Church in Janesville, Wis., and three years at Trinity Episcopal Church in Wauwatosa, Wis., where I served as Sunday Assistant and teacher of the adult classes. My thanks are due to the people who attended the classes and taught me so much, and to the rectors of the two parishes, the Rev. Ronald Ortmeyer and the Rev. Kenneth E. Trueman. I am grateful also to the Rev. Canon James R. Brown, Warden of St. John's College, Winnipeg, who invited me to give a series of lectures on this method to the clergy of the Diocese of Rupertsland. The Rt. Rev. Albert W. Hillestad and the Rev. Prof. Merrill Abbey were kind enough to read all or parts of the manuscript and to make helpful suggestions. Mrs. Karen Gildersleeve was kind enough to transcribe the tape of the discussion in Example 15 and Mrs. Terry Koehler assisted in preparing the entire manuscript for publication; only this notice keeps those tasks from being thankless. I wish to convey my appreciation to the Rev. Carroll Simcox, editor of *The Living Church*, for permission to use here material that had an earlier life in articles in that magazine.

Contents

The Living and Active Word

Introduction

What follows is a "how-to-do-it" book on preaching that gives a step-by-step method for constructing sermons that relate the Bible seriously to the challenge of being a Christian in today's world. The method has been developed by the writer in his weekly efforts as a seminary professor of New Testament to show the members of a suburban congregation the implications of the gospel for their lives. It is based on several convictions:

1. To be Christian, preaching must be biblical.

2. The only valid interpretation of the Bible today is historical, critical interpretation.

3. To have more than antiquarian interest, the Bible has to be correlated with real issues in the life of today.

4. The Word of God cannot be told from on high, but must be spoken in conversation and expect a reply.

When these convictions are put together as requirements for a sermon, they result in a simple pattern for a one-point sermon that can be followed easily. The method cannot guarantee to make a Chrysostom, a golden-tongued speaker for God, out of all who use it, but it can make sure that those who follow it will attempt honestly to explore what the Spirit has to say to the Churches; for many that will be a darned sight more than they are doing now.

The book is divided into two parts, roughly equal in length. In the first half the reader is taken through the successive steps involved in preparing a sermon by this method. These are: (1) discovering what the sacred writers are trying to say in the passages of Scripture that will be read at the service for which the sermon is designed, (2) finding out what situation in the life of the congregation (whether at a personal, parochial, or national level) is an appropriate context in which to affirm the point that the sacred text makes, (3) structuring the sermon in such a way that the hearers will have the aspect of their lives about which you preach illuminated by the appointed biblical passage, and (4) delivering the sermon in the manner and under the conditions that are most propitious for getting the message across.

The second half of the book will consist of sermons prepared according to the method by the author. They are limited to his own work, not because it is so eloquent or edifying, but only because it provides convenient illustrations of aspects of the method. They are—for better or worse—not even sermons that you can tinker with slightly and preach yourself; each was written for a particular congregation at a certain moment in its history and is already dated by the time that it is published. They are included solely because they illustrate the principles that have been discussed. For that reason, the most useful part of the second half will not be the sermons themselves but the accompanying explanatory notes that call attention to the sermons as cases in point of suggestions made in the first half of the book.

It should be stated explicitly that even the author knows that this is not the only legitimate way to preach from the Bible today; the subtitle describes it as "a way" to preach from the Bible today. One of my friends says that the surest demonstration of the truth of the Christian religion is that it has survived twenty centuries of preaching. It is true that many clergy appear to have a Midas touch in reverse, being able to turn the exciting and life-giving gold of the gospel into a dull and deadly dross that is base metal indeed. This book is written in the hope that it will help some preachers to reverse the trend, so that they will show once again that the word of God is living and active and sharper than a two-edged sword.

Method

PART I

How to Hear What the Biblical Writer Is Saying

Among the half-dozen or so books I have read that have changed my life is one that was written a few years ago by James D. Smart, who taught biblical interpretation at Union Theological Seminary in New York. Its title is *The Strange Silence of the Bible in the Church: A Study in Hermeneutics*. In it Smart points out that most sermons show very little effect of the many hours' study of biblical criticism their preachers engaged in while in seminary. The reason, he suggests, is a gap in the curriculum of seminaries. Biblical interpretation is taught by one group of professors and homiletics is taught by another. The biblical scholars assume that their job has been done when they have taught their students how to discover what the sacred writers intended their original readers to understand. Teachers of preaching assume that their students know how to draw on the Bible as a resource for preaching and so limit their instruction to the preparation and delivery of sermons. No one ever teaches the fledgling clergyman how to apply the Bible to the lives of their people today. That falls between the two academic chairs of Bible and Preaching. And, since no one ever taught clergy how to draw on the insights into the meaning of the Bible that they acquired in their exegetical courses as a resource for their preaching, they do not do so. Most clergy I know preach like functional Fundamentalists. No one would ever learn from one of their sermons that they have any doubts about the plenary verbal inspiration of the Bible.

These shortcomings in seminary training have two effects. The first is on the preacher himself. His critical knowledge has undermined his confidence in the surface meaning of the text, and he is too conscientious to preach as though he were unaware of the problem. At the same time, no one has taught him how to share what he believes the Bible really means, and so he hesitates to try that. The result is that his preaching usually says little about the Bible. The second effect is on his hearers. Many of them probably have the same kind of problems with the literal meaning of the text that he does and are left to feel guilty or bored. His preaching has done nothing to show them that the Bible is the Christian's key to understanding what his life and the world are all about. The result is that the Bible is silent in the Church.

As I said, Smart's book changed my life. It made me determined that my exegetical classes would not stop short with what the New Testament writings meant to their original audience, but would go on to explore how that meaning could be applied to life today. This book is an extension of that project.

Someone could ask, however, why it matters that the Bible is silent in the Church, that sermons are not based on its texts. Certainly the question is worth asking. When we think that one of the Twelve Apostles wrote something or that Jesus himself actually said a particular thing in so many words, we have one attitude toward it. When instead we refer vaguely to tradition formed within the community of the primitive Church, we have quite a different attitude. Further, we have had the experience of seeing the biblical worldview upset by our own observation. More than thirty years ago Rudolf Bultmann made a statement that has since become classic: "It is impossible to use electric light and the wireless and to avail ourselves of modern medical and surgical discoveries, and at the same time to believe in the New Testament world of spirits and miracles." [1] To an age that has seen the landing of a spaceship on the moon on live TV, Bultmann's references to "wireless" and electric lights seem about as quaint as the belief in demons and nature miracles looked to him.

What is it in the Bible that makes it appropriate for the Christian community to read from it at almost all of its meetings, and for the clergyman to base addresses to those meetings on its interpretation, claiming that it is the source of all the community's doctrines? Or, to phrase the matter differently, how can contemporary Episcopalians continue to affirm as one of their Articles of Religion the statement that was drawn up 400 years ago:

Holy Scripture containeth all things necessary to salvation: so that whatsoever is not read therein, nor may be proved thereby, is not to be required of any man, that it should be believed as an article of the Faith, or be thought requisite or necessary to salvation?

The best answer to this question that I have seen is given by the Scottish Old Testament scholar, James Barr. He points out that to be Christian a theology must give a central place to Jesus of Nazareth and that its God must be the God who was known in Israel. The Israelite knowledge of God is thus the classic model. That model was formulated in an ongoing and changing tradition which was at first oral but was later fixed in writing. Once written, the tradition began to "curve back on itself" and thus to take on an authoritative position. In this manner it became the classic model. Thus "the centrality of the Bible is the recognition of the classic sources for the expression of Jesus and God." [2]

All right, so the Bible is our classic source for knowledge of God and Jesus, but how reliable is it? Without even asking questions about the "quest of the historical Jesus," one can see that a number of elements in the biblical understanding of God are, according to our notion, simply mistaken. To give but one kind of example, the Second Isaiah was wrong in believing that God would return all the exiles from Babylon to Israel, Paul was wrong in believing that God would cause the Jews to become so jealous of the gentiles' enjoyment of the kingdom that they would be converted, and the author of the Revelation was wrong in expecting the immediate end of the Roman empire. Barr also has what I think is the correct response to the insight that there are theological imperfections in the Bible: "The status of the Bible is one of sufficiency rather than of perfection." [3] Whatever its imperfections, the Bible still is entirely adequate to fulfill its purpose of being the classic source for our knowledge of Jesus and the Israelite experience of God. If it distresses us to think of the Bible as imperfect, perhaps we can console ourselves with the thought that the Bible we have is the one God gave us. It is presumptuous of us to think that we ought to have something better than he chose to give. Because we are convinced that the Bible comes from God in a deeper sense than all other created things do, we have to believe that it is the best Bible possible.

Because the Bible is the classic and adequate source of our knowledge about Jesus and the religious experience of Israel, it serves as the criterion by which our own beliefs are to be evaluated. This does not mean, of course, that the correct theological method for today consists of extrapolating theological statements from the Holy Scriptures and correlating them systematically. The theological and philosophical vocabularies of today are very different from those of the more than 2,000 years in which the biblical tradition was being created and written down. Our theology has to be in our own vocabulary; it has to be a part of what Peter Berger and Thomas Luckmann have designated as our own "social construction of reality." [4] But the Bible remains the norm by which the Christianity of our theology is evaluated. Our continuity with the biblical community is documented by the conformity of our thought to the classic model. Again, Barr says it neatly: "The relation between the man of the Bible with his situation and the man of today with his modern situation is provided by two things: That they are in the continuity of the one people of God and that their faith is related to the biblical model of understanding." [5] Thus the reason that we preach from the Bible today is to make certain that our contemporary Christian proclamation is consonant with its classic model.

Having said that the Bible is "the classic source for the expression of Jesus and God," we still have not shown what it is in the Bible that we look for. This point can be clarified by reference to a letter once sent to me. It asked:

How do we distinguish what is cultural from what is revelation in holy scripture? I think this issue underlies several subjects currently under debate. Marriage canons: were the views of Christ and St. Paul on marriage and family merely cultural expressions, or were they revelation of the God-ordained order for marriage and family? Women priests: were there no such persons in the scripture because of the cultural prohibitions, or because this was the way God ordained things to be? Priorities in the mission of the church: should the proclamation of the Word be primary or was that merely a cultural priority based on the presupposition of a pagan culture which had never heard of this new Christianity? What about the role of ordained leaders in the church—deacons to serve and meet needs of poor and widows while elders give themselves to prayer and teaching: is this merely first century, or is it the plan of God for all times?

The main issue here is the content of revelation. What is revealed in revelation? To indicate the variety of possible answers to this question, we can look at two that most contemporary churchmen would find unacceptable. The first of these is the opinion of many Jews in our Lord's time and for a number of centuries afterwards that what was revealed in the scripture was God's religious regulations. The Old Testament was treated as a legal code that was to be combed in search of all the rules in it. These were extracted and codified first in oral tradition, then in the Mishnah, and later in the Talmud. The content of revelation was legal in their understanding.

Another way of identifying the content of revelation is that of the Fundamentalist. His essential attitude toward the Bible has been excellently described by Robert S. Ellwood, Jr.:

Bible time is special; it stands in equal relation to all other points in time. The evangelical is always contemporaneous with it, particularly with the time of Christ. He always wants to collapse into nothing all time between himself and the New Testament. He strives to negate all customs and attitudes which have evolved in the life of the church between then and now. He wants to walk into the time capsule which is the New Testament world, with its miracles, its expectation of an immediate end, and above all the mighty tangible presence of Jesus Christ. He wants to be the thirteenth disciple and to write in his own life the twenty-ninth chapter of the Book of Acts.[6]

This attitude toward the Bible makes it possible for the Fundamentalist to regard the content of revelation as directions to him for the conduct of his life in each concrete situation in which he finds himself. The biblical words need no interpretation, application, or translation into other categories to be immediately relevant and usable.

These two unacceptable designations of what it is that revelation is supposed to reveal have been offered to show that a number of different opinions on the subject have been held by various people at various times and that, therefore, the content of revelation cannot be understood as something that has always been recognized and agreed upon by everyone. That paves the way for saying that there is a history to the interpretation of the Bible that stretches back to the time that the material in it was first written down—and in some cases stretches back even further than that since the material in question was passed down by word of mouth for a long time before it was fixed in writing. The most universally accepted interpretation of the Bible today, however, is historical interpretation. It asks what the sacred writer intended his first readers to understand. This is to say that the writings in the Bible were not originally set down as Holy Scripture that would be eternally valid, but were originally a response of the writer to a situation that he had encountered. He wrote to communicate an attitude toward that situation. The continuing validity of the Bible depends on there being an analogy between the situations back then to which the sacred words were originally intended to speak and the situations of our lives. If the situations are similar, then we may legitimately expect that there can also be a transfer of the attitude from the ancient situation to the modern one.

Our ability to discover the ancient situation has been greatly increased by the discovery of biblical scholars that there is a relation between the way that a passage was constructed and the kind of situation in which it was used, between the form and the purpose of the passage. In the New Testament the purposes of all the writings can be summarized as either convincing people that Jesus of Nazareth was of ultimate significance for their lives or showing them that accepting that conviction has implications for the practical way in which they lived their lives. Both purposes were an aspect of what we call "preaching" in English, but note that by "preaching" we may refer either to evangelism or to moral exhortation. These two kinds of preaching are sometimes referred to as *proclamation* (in Greek, *kerygma*) and *parenesis* (the transliteration of a Greek word that means exhortation).

While proclamation and *parenesis* are the major forms of all New Testament writings, each of them can be broken down into a number of sub-forms, each of which indicates something of the situation in which it was originally used. The letters of St. Paul, for instance, were originally his response to a practical situation that had arisen in one of the missionary churches that he had founded. When he could not go and settle the matter in person, he did the next best thing and dashed off a letter that said what he would have said in person if he could have been there. The first thing to be noticed about that is that the applicability of what he said then to our life today depends on the similarity of our situation to the one to which he was responding. The next thing to be noticed is that the form of these letters was *parenesis*. Finally, we can notice a third thing: that in writing these letters, Paul did not make up everything he said, but incorporated into them many quotations that he borrowed from other sources. Some he borrowed from the liturgy, such as hymns, confessions, benedictions, and so forth, but others came from sources such as lists of virtues and vices, tables of the duties of members of a household, and passages from the Old Testament. These borrowed elements, then, have two situations in which they were used: the situation from which Paul borrowed them and that in which he employed them. Both need to be considered in transferring the application of these passages to life today.

While the form of the Pauline letters is *parenesis*, the

form of the gospels is proclamation. This was well stated by the author of the Fourth Gospel (who used the overall form in common with the authors of the synoptic gospels, although he did not use the same sub-forms): "These are written that you may believe that Jesus is the Christ, the Son of God, and that believing you may have life in his name" (John 20:31). The gospels, too, have numerous sub-forms that indicate to us the situation in the early Church to which that particular sort of story was applied. These sub-forms include stories that lead us to an authoritative statement by Jesus as the dramatic "punchline," stories that relate some miracle performed by Jesus either in healing or in some triumph over nature, parables, and many others. Most of these have as their basic purpose the proclamation of salvation in Jesus, but there are variations in the way they express it, so we need to take that into account when we transfer their meaning to life today.

Just as we saw that not all of St. Paul's material originated with him, we should also see that there is a history to the material used in the gospels before its incorporation into the biblical books in which we know it. The stories that relate historical incidents derive in their first level from the life and ministry of Jesus. A situation there, then, is their primary level of meaning. Their secondary level of meaning is in the context of the situation in the early Church in which it appeared appropriate and useful to preserve and pass down that particular story. The third level of meaning would be the use that is made of it by the evangelist in whose gospel it appears. He may see a situation to which that story is relevant that looks very different from either its situation in the life of Jesus or the situation in the early Church in which it was passed down by word of mouth. At this third level of meaning we recognize that stories in Matthew and Luke may also have an earlier appearance and meaning in either Mark or the sayings collection called "Q" or the special source of that evangelist. Here again, all of the three situations will have to be considered when we transfer the application of these passages to life today.

What we have said about the way to discover what the Bible reveals about the meaning of our life today is that we should seek to locate the situation in which each passage in the Bible was originally written and then find the most analogous situation in our contemporary life. The attitude toward that situation in the text may then be transferred to the modern situation. We have seen that we need the aid of modern scholarly techniques of biblical study to uncover the situation to which the passage was originally addressed. It should be pointed out that the same sort of aid is necessary in understanding the attitude toward the situation that is expressed in the Bible. It was expressed in ancient thought forms that in their surface meaning could be very misleading to a modern person interested in the meaning of the Bible. This is to say that all proper biblical interpreters today must use the historical critical method if they wish to understand what the sacred writers intended to communicate to their first readers. In other words, we must engage in exegesis, which has been defined by Willi Marxsen as "the repetition in my language of what an author wanted to say to his readers." [7]

Everything we have said up to this point has been leading up to one simple statement: The first step in preparing a sermon is to exegete the biblical passage from which you are to preach. When you are following a lectionary of appointed lessons for each Sunday and holy day, you will obviously preach from one of those lessons. Sometimes you will not decide which one to preach from until you have done at least preliminary exegesis of all of them, waiting for something to strike you as appropriate to your congregation at that time.

This brings us to much the same sort of situation as that

of the famous recipe for tiger stew that begins, "First you catch a tiger. . . ." The beginning part is the hard part. How does one exegete the passage? There are, of course, short cuts. One could merely open a handy one-volume commentary to its treatment of the passage and see what it has to say, or, with even less labor, consult one of several exegetical and homiletical guides to each week's lections. Either of those practices is far better than nothing, but both fall considerably short of offering the value of making one's own study of the passage. With these short aids you get the results of exegesis without the process, and often you do not know the significance of the results unless you have gone through the process. At any rate, the scholar who prepared the aids went through all the steps of exegesis and anyone who makes use of his work will do so more wisely if he knows how the scholar went about it. The steps are the same whether you do them yourself or let someone do them for you. The steps that I will describe, though, are not an impossible ideal, but represent what any pastor can do if he spends an hour each morning studying for his sermon and then gives over Saturday morning for the actual writing of it.

The first step in interpreting a biblical passage is, not very surprisingly, reading it carefully. Ideally this means reading it in its original language. The next best thing to doing that is to read it thoughtfully and comparatively in several different translations. Often that can give you a sense of the range of meanings in the original. It can also give you a range of ways of saying something that you may want to call on in the actual writing of the sermon.

The next step is to discover the exact words that the sacred writer wrote. Remember that the New Testament was preserved in handwritten manuscripts for almost a millennium and a half before printing began. The most careful copyist makes some mistakes, whether intentional or unintentional, so no two manuscripts were ever exactly alike. All of these countless variations leave some questions about the original phrasing of the passage. While none of these variants brings into question any basic issue of the faith, some of them do cast very different lights on the meaning of a particular passage. To find out what the biblical author meant, you have to start with finding what he said. If you are working from the Greek, the task is relatively easy in that you do have the alternatives clearly before you. English readers will never learn of many of the variants, because most are never indicated on the printed page. Even here, though, the task is not utterly impossible. Most of the modern translations will have the truly significant variants listed in a footnote at the bottom of the page with some such introduction as, "Other ancient authorities read" or "add" whatever the different reading is.

After the text has been established as well as possible, you must look up in a Bible dictionary everything mentioned in the passage that you are not familiar with. If a character is mentioned, find out what else is known about him and how what is said here squares with that. If a place is mentioned, learn about it. Units of measure often need to be checked. Certainly amounts of money do; modern translators often wish to state the equivalent in buying power in their own coinage, which can lead to very misleading figures after there has been a little time for devaluation to occur. Checking references to living conditions is often very illuminating; e.g., the parable of the sower makes much more sense when one knows that in Palestine sowing was done before plowing.

Not only do you need to check out persons, places, and things, you also need to check out the theological vocabulary. Many key words are used very differently by different writers and none of their meanings is likely to be precisely the same as the popular modern use of the same word. St. Paul and the author of the Epistle of James do not mean the same thing by "faith," for instance, and neither of them means by it what the author of Hebrews does. A good theological dictionary of the Bible can be very helpful in discovering what a technical term means in the passage you are studying.

This reference to the different ways different authors use a term calls our attention to the fact that the passages we study do not exist in splendid isolation but are part of a book. Our passages form one link in the chain of that book's total argument. This means that in order to understand the passage fully, we must understand it as part of a whole. Doing so involves seeing what comes before and what comes after our section, but it also involves a good bit more. It involves questions of who wrote the book, when, where, why, and to whom. These are what scholars refer to as questions of introduction and they are best answered by consulting one of the good scholarly introductions to the Old or New Testament. Often commentaries also have introductory sections that precede their verse-by-verse analysis; this is true of single-volume commentaries on the whole Bible as well as volumes devoted to individual books. Learning what the author is trying to say with his entire book makes it much easier to understand what he is trying to say in our particular passage.

We have seen above that some biblical books draw on sources. This is the stage of the investigation at which those should be checked into. The introduction will have called attention to them if there are any. Sources in the Old Testament are a rather complicated matter, but they are less so in the New Testament. Outside of Old Testament quotations and liturgical fragments, 2 Peter's use of Jude is the only major dependence on a source outside of the synoptic gospels. For all practical purposes, then, when we speak of checking sources, we are talking about the synoptics. In dealing with them we are lucky in having a tool that greatly simplifies the task of investigating sources. We can get a synopsis of the gospels in Greek or English that has the versions of the same story in the different gospels set side-by-side in parallel columns. (That, of course, is why they are called synoptic: they can be seen together [Greek: *synoptikos*].) By comparing the versions thus we can see what is unique to each and what is shared with one or more of the other gospels. Anything in common with Mark may be thought to be derived from Mark. Anything that Matthew and Luke share that is missing from Mark is attributed to the Q source. Everything that is peculiar to Matthew or Luke was either derived by the author from his special source or is a result of his editing of Mark or Q. We will discuss below the use that is to be made of this information about sources.

The next step is to see what type of literature our passage represents. We are able to recognize various types of literature by their pattern or structure. When, for example, we read a poem that is fourteen lines long and each of those lines is ten syllables in length and the stress falls on the second of alternating syllables and the rhyme scheme is of an established pattern, we know that the poem is a sonnet. While we would find it a little more difficult to state the specifications of a novel, we generally know when we have read one. Oral literature falls into similar patterns. The easiest way to demonstrate that in our society is to look at one of our largest bodies of oral literature, jokes. We could easily draw up the specifications of elephant jokes, shaggy dog stories, "some good news and some bad news" gags, "knock-knock" jokes and so on. The person trained to do so can do equally well in describing and recognizing the forms of literature appearing in the Bible, many of which were oral forms before they were written. The study of these forms is called "form criticism." It is very important to New Testament exegesis because, as we have seen above, the literary form used is often one of our surest guides to the purpose of the author. I must have recognized this early and instinctively, because as a youth I courted a girl with limericks, knowing that she was bound to be flattered, but could not take them too seriously. Form, then, is one of our best indicators of the situation in which a story was used.

By and large the use of form criticism (in dealing with the gospels, at any rate) is limited to the individual story since the form of the gospel as a whole is, as we saw above, proclamation. Since the form of all the larger units is the same, our knowledge is not advanced by identifying it. This fits in with our knowledge of how the gospels came to be written, because we know that long before they were incorporated into written accounts of the life of Jesus, the individual stories were passed down separately by word of mouth in the Christian community. The work of the gospel writers, then, was to string the separate stories together into a continuous narrative. Mark, of course, took his stories over from oral tradition, but Matthew and Luke drew on their sources of Mark, Q, and their own special material. The evangelists, though, are not to be thought of as if they put together nothing but what had been passed down to them so that their assembled gospels show no personal influences. This "untouched by human hands" view of the construction of a gospel is quite misleading. To begin with, the order in which they put the stories together makes some difference in the meaning of the whole. Not only that, but when we do source analysis, we see that there are changes in the way that a story is told that do not suggest so much that the gospel writer is drawing on outside information as that he is deliberately rewriting it to express a point of view. The next stage of exegesis after form criticism, then, is a study of the editing that the particular evangelist did when he included a passage in his gospel. This study of the editorial activity is called "redaction criticism." This editing is our guide to the gospel writer's attitude toward the situation for which he is writing. We ask why he changed this detail and that one and why he put this story where he did, and we begin to get some idea of his purpose in writing.

Perhaps you have had the experience of visiting an English cathedral that includes in its structure almost the entire history of English architecture. The crypt may be Saxon and the nave Norman, the choir Decorated and the sanctuary Perpendicular, while the rood screen is Jacobite and the baptistry Victorian. The same kind of indications of period in a gospel story are obvious to a trained eye. One can detect which elements go back to the ministry of Jesus, which were added during the time the story was handed down by word of mouth, which came from the hand of Mark, and which from a later gospel writer. When we have gone through all of the steps in exegesis that we have been listing, we ought to be able to do that with our passage. We should then be able to identify the situation which the passage was addressed to at every stage of its history, and we should be able to say what the attitude toward that situation was. Thus we have found what in the passage may be applied to contemporary life.

Just to make sure that we have understood it all correctly, though, our last step in exegesis will be to check our findings with those of good, reliable, modern commentaries on the book with which we have been working. If there are marked differences between the commentator's findings and ours, there are two possible explanations: (1) we may have slipped up somewhere and should go back and check over our work, or (2) we may have made a great advance in biblical understanding and should write up our results for a scholarly journal.

How to Hear What Your Congregation Is Saying about Itself

Having seen how we discover what the situation in the text is, our next task is to find out how we isolate the corresponding situation in our congregation. Before we do that, however, we need first to assure ourselves that the effort to do so is legitimate. To an extent we have already done this when we inquired into what is authoritative about the Bible. We said that it is the classic source of information about Jesus and the Israelite experience of God. As Christians we are the people who are in continuity with the communities that wrote the Bible and we consider this classic statement about Jesus and God to be normative for us. If we stand in the same relation to Jesus and the Father as the communities to whom the biblical writings were addressed, we may expect to find ourselves in many of the same situations, and there should be a valid carry-over from them to us.

Modern theologians have a number of ways of talking about this correspondence between the situation in the biblical text and the situation in the life of the Church today. One important example is that of the New

Hermeneutic. This school of theology makes use of concepts it has borrowed from the thought of the German philosopher Martin Heidegger. Heidegger regards serious writing as a self-disclosure of Being to the writer. The disclosure occurs not by way of the writer's arriving at a concept and then expressing it in appropriate language, because the concept does not exist indepdently of the language in which it is couched. To say that one has a thought that he cannot put into words is to say that he has no thought at all, or at best an ill-formed one. Instead, the concept is formed in the very process of phrasing it. For an author to write a truth is for him to discover and even, to an extent, create that truth. Heidegger calls such a "coming into language" of a truth a "Word Event" (*Wortereignis*, in German). Now the point is that all Word Events are not those of writers. Readers also experience Word Events. When they repeat the experience and understanding of the author, they re-create the formation of the concept and undergo a Word Event. Or, more properly, they repeat the Word Event of the author.

The path by which Christians appropriate Heidegger's understanding is obvious enough. Although Heidegger himself has proclaimed the "end of metaphysics" and could be classified as an atheist, one who does believe in God could easily understand the Being that discloses itself in Word Events to be the God of Jews and Christians, who reveals himself to his people. The Sacred Scriptures are thus seen to be Word Events in which the truth that God reveals about himself has come into language. The original writing is the primary Word Event, but the exegete's interpretation of what was written is an effort to repeat that Word Event and the preacher's proclamation is an attempt to arrange for the congregation to repeat it again.

It is worth the time to express this insight in the

language of those with whom it originated. Let us begin with Gerhard Ebeling's definition of the word of God:

God's word is not various things, but one single thing—the word that makes man human by making him a believer, i.e., a man who confesses to God as his future and therefore does not fail his fellow men in the one absolutely necessary and salutary thing, *viz.*, true word.[1]

This one word of God, however, is embodied in a number of different biblical texts. Each of the biblical texts was preaching in its original state; we recognized this in the first chapter when we said that the form of all New Testament writing is either proclamation or *parenesis*, which are two types of preaching. Thus Manfred Mezger said of these texts: "They once *were* preaching, they *are* preaching; essentially, therefore, they can again *'become'* preaching today." [2] Or, to quote Ebeling again,

The process from text to sermon can therefore be characterized by saying: Proclamation that has taken place is to become proclamation that takes place. The transition from text to sermon is a transition from Scripture to the spoken word. Thus the task prescribed here consists in making what is written into spoken word or, as we can now also say, in letting the text become God's word again.[3]

This does not mean, however, that all the preacher has to do is to say the same words over. Our hearers today are not in the same historical situation that the first hearers were in, but are in a comparable situation. They must be shown how their situation corresponds to that in the text. "Translating does not mean simply to substitute one word for another, but to seek and find at once the new place at which this text, without detriment to its historical individuality, meets us." [4] By so doing, the preacher builds a bridge between the situation in the text and the situation in the congregation. Indeed, this hermeneutical bridge is one that has a number of arches: that which spans from the writer to the exegete, that from the exegete to the preacher, that from the preacher to his congregation in church, and that from the lives of the congregation in church to their lives in the world. In each case, however, it is a correspondence of situation that makes it possible for the Word Event to be repeated, for the hermeneutical arch to be constructed.

Another useful way of talking about this comes from Paul Tillich's discussion of the theological method that he used himself and that he claims has always been used by theology, whether consciously or not. This method is to be preferred to several inadequate methods such as the supernaturalistic (that "takes the Christian message to be a sum of revealed truths which have fallen into the human situation like strange bodies from a strange world"), the naturalistic or humanistic (in which "the contents of the Christian faith were explained as man's religious self-realization in the progressive process of religious history"), and the dualistic (that "builds a supranatural structure on a natural substructure").[5] The correct method that Tillich recommends is the method of correlation. Briefly stated, this method attempts to correlate the questions implied in every aspect of human existence with answers supplied in revelation. Indeed, the very questions that life poses are seen as evidence that life does not answer its own questions. Its failure to do so implies that answers come from beyond the·human situation; they come, in fact, from God. As Tillich himself phrased it:

In using the method of correlation, systematic theology pro-ceeds in the following way: it makes an analysis of the human situation out of which the existential questions arise, and it demonstrates that the symbols used in the Christian message are the answers of those questions.[6]

What is correlated, then, is life today and the biblical

revelation, if one may oversimplify. When we state the matter this way, though, it becomes obvious that Tillich sought in his whole theological enterprise to do what we have said is the task of the preacher from week to week. He undertook to paint the total picture while we contract for small details, but the principle is the same. His techniques for identifying the questions implicit in the human situation today are thus likely to be useful to us.

"The analysis of the human situation," he tells us,

employs materials made available by man's creative self-interpretation in all realms of culture. Philosophy contributes, but so do poetry, drama, the novel, therapeutic psychology, and sociology.[7]

Elsewhere Tillich makes quite explicit the bond between the tasks of theology and preaching and the common methodological ground they share:

So far as my own thinking and preaching are concerned—especially preaching, which is more important ultimately than theology—I have found that my relationship to the visual arts and to drama and poetry and the novel has made it possible for me to offer fresh interpretations of the Christian symbols. . . . But we should be careful about one thing: we should not confuse the artistic symbolization of religious symbols with the religious symbols themselves, thus implying that art can replace religion.[8]

Although he recognizes that psychology and sociology can offer tools for diagnosing the human condition, we notice that he looks especially to the arts to disclose our existential questions. The reason that the arts furnish an even better barometer for gauging the preoccupations of man than the human sciences can be demonstrated simply by a reference to fashion designers. It is generally admitted that their work is one of the more trivial of the arts, yet even they possess a quality common to all artists. That quality is a sensitivity to what people are thinking and feeling. Artists anticipate the directions in which society moves. Fashion designers, for instance, seem to know what colors the world is ready to appreciate again. I cannot believe that the way that one season many new clothes will be one color and the next season they will be another is just part of a gigantic capitalist plot to separate people from their money by selling them clothes they do not need for the protection of their bodies. While one must allow for elements of greed, the fact remains that we all are prepared again to celebrate the glories of magenta or chartreuse or whatever the "in" color happens to be that season. The designers anticipate our values because they experience the appreciation we are ready to give before we do and they tell us correctly that the current color is the one we are ripe for. This capacity for feeling what we are going to feel before we feel it is one quality that all artists have in common. Thus, when we look at their works we see a mirror in which we can behold ourselves. The artist's intuitive sense of where society is often is more reliable than the careful empirical studies of scientists.

Tillich's awareness of the value of the arts for displaying the human condition has launched an entire theological discipline. While it is an exaggeration to say that the theological interpretation of literature is the invention of Nathan A. Scott, Jr., Scott has revived that particular critical approach in recent years. In the preface to his first book, Scott gives an account of how he came to get the idea of doing a theological criticism of literature. The basis for such an undertaking is the realization that "the theological community must . . . enter into a dialogical relation with philosophy, with the social sciences, with therapeutic psychology, with imaginative literature—and it must do this because of the very nature of Christian theology itself." Scott goes on to say, "It was this recognition (toward which I was greatly assisted by Professor Tillich) that marked a decisive stage in the development of my own theological thought." [9] It will be noticed that the aspect of Tillich's work to which Scott calls attention is precisely the method of correlation that, as we have seen, has a marked applicability to the work of the preacher. This means that, as we shall see later in more detail, the arts offer the preacher some of his best insights into the situation in the pew to which he must link up the situation in the biblical text.

Before we list the sources from which we derive our insights into the situation of man today, however, we have to say something about the way we determine that a contemporary situation corresponds to the situation in the biblical passage from which we are preaching. Here we are getting into a matter that is very difficult to express and the only way that I know to say what I want is to resort to an analogy.

When I was a boy, my friends and I spent all of our available time in constructing model airplanes. We not only made flying models that were constructed much like real aircraft, but we also made solid models out of blocks of balsa wood. These blocks had to be carved and sanded until they were the shape of the outline on the plan. Since the models were three-dimensional, the shaping had to be correct for the end as well as for the side view. In fact, it had to be right for every cross-section along the length of the fuselage. To make it possible for us to measure these cross-sections and make sure they were the correct size, the plans always included some templates. These were usually printed rectangles on the plans from which the correct shape of the particular cross-section was deleted. These templates could be cut out (I don't recall that I ever actually did that, though) and held against the model to see if the shaping was right at that particular spot.

After growing up I learned that there are templates for all kinds of things, and it seems to me that templates offer one of the best analogies to the way the Bible reveals to us the meaning of our existence and experience. The situations that arise in the biblical narratives or that are commented on by the prophets, apostles, and our Lord can function as templates for us. By holding various ones up to our situation, we find the situation that matches and apply to it the understanding given the situation in the Bible. Or we can work in the opposite direction, as we do in preaching, holding up the biblical template and measuring against it the various situations of our life until we find one that matches.

The analogy of the template has the disadvantage that it is a static image for a dynamic relation and thus it appears to take the life out of the reality to which it alludes. Perhaps, though, it is not so inadequate as it first appears. The templates provided in my model airplane kits for the cross-sections of wings were just the delineations of shapes on paper, but for the physicist specializing in aerodynamics who designed these airfoils, they represented highly complex balances of mathematical formulae by which the forces of lift and drag could be so related as to permit the plane to fly. In the templates of biblical revelation, the shape is the product of a dynamic interplay of forces.

The problem for the preacher, though, is finding the contemporary situation that matches the biblical template. The way he does that is to know as much as he can about what is going on in his world and to be as familiar with it as he can. This way he will be aware of many of the situations in which his people live. He holds up the biblical template and tests the situations he thinks might match against the template. The technique will be largely one of free association. After he has determined what the situation of the text is, he will ask himself which situations in the congregation correspond to it. He will then compare the most likely candidates until he finds one that matches. That is what he will preach on.

In order to make that work, he will need to be like the beasts in the book of Revelation, "all eyes within," and will need a great number on the outside as well. As my old preaching professor in seminary, James T. Cleland, used to say, "The preacher should have a homiletical eye and a homiletical ear, but not a homiletical mouth." Another way of saying the same thing is that the preacher is a hermeneut, an interpreter, not only of the biblical text, but also of his congregation and society. He needs not only to understand what is going on in the world himself, but also to be able to help others to understand it. And the way he will know that is to look and listen at everything that goes on around him and to reflect on it in the light of the gospel. Then he will have something to preach about.

In the first place, he will listen directly to his parishioners. There are three main situations in which he will do this: visiting, counseling, and hearing confessions. The minister needs some way of getting to know his people in a relaxed and informal way so that if a crisis arises they will wish to call on him and he will know to whom he is ministering when they call. In my own parochial ministry, which was admittedly some time ago and in small parishes, that personal familiarity was acquired through visiting. It was in this situation that I became aware of what they were all about, what made them tick. Their degree of involvement in the church program, what they liked and did not like about what was going on in the parish, their own religious commitment and experience all came out in these visits. Many other things also came out that were not so obviously churchy, but which were far more significant indicators of where their souls were. Their attitudes toward their houses and the furnishing of them, for instance, told me a lot about what their personal value systems were. Their feelings about their jobs, their children, and world affairs came out in ways that were both direct and indirect. If preaching is for the purpose of helping Christian people understand their lives in the light of the gospel, the preacher must know the aspects of his parishioners' lives they are trying to understand. Visiting is one of the best ways to find this out and is, therefore, one of the most important resources the minister has for preaching.

Since counseling deals with problem areas, it provides a sharp focus for the preacher's inquiry into the situation of his congregation. Of course, one should never preach in such a way that he appears to have violated the confidentiality of the counseling relation, but one can draw on what he learns from his counseling in a general way that permits him to preach about what he knows are real issues in the congregation. This *can* be done without making anyone feel that his personal linen is being laundered in a detergent commercial on TV. I remember the discussion that followed a sermon I preached on the crisis of the middle years, in which many marriages are endangered. One of the parishioners questioned the reality of the problem, saying that most of the friends his wife and he had were in that age bracket, and they were not aware of such frictions in any of those marriages. The rector of the parish was able to say what number of counseling sessions of all sorts he had conducted during the previous month and what proportion of those sessions had dealt with just such problems. The percentage was dramatically high and demonstrated conclusively that the problem was not only real in the society at large, as the sociological data I had presented had shown, but was also acute in that very congregation. It also showed that the rector was aware of what kinds of problems his people were dealing with and was thus in a position to preach to real needs when it was his turn in the pulpit. Far too many sermons are spent answering unasked questions when one considers the superabundance of real questions that get asked in the crisis counseling that a minister does.

Private confession is a practice that has not been common in many Christian bodies, and it suffered a decline in the years after Vatican II in the communions in which it had a more established place. But the preacher who hears confessions has an advantage that other clergy lack by the unique access confession gives him to the deepest spiritual concerns of his people. By this I do not mean especially the information he thus acquires about which commandments are being broken by his parishioners. Years ago in Bruce Marshall's novel, Father Smith complained mildly that the sins confessed are "un-original." No, it has been my experience that it is sometimes in the confessional that people mention the things which are in their hearts and on their consciences and which they would not mention under any other circumstances. The little things that people worry about in the middle of the night come out there. People who appear to have great inner calm and security show themselves to have been tormented over a period of years by something which, from the point of view of moral theology, need never have bothered them. (If it appears that my reference to the difference between the way people look and the way they see themselves betrays a breach of the anonymity of the confessional, I can only say that in parishes the size of mine anonymity of the confessional could only be a convention. More importantly, however, I never indicated out of the confessional what I had learned there, even though there was no way I could not have known which of my few parishioners who were regular penitents was addressing me in that familiar voice.) When some of these hidden griefs and these unnecessary feelings of guilt can be relieved anonymously from the pulpit, the preacher's message will be gospel indeed.

Not all of the listening the preacher needs to do, however, is to his parishioners. Although there are times when it may look like we and they inhabit parochial ghettos, we are inextricably members of a larger society. To document that point, we need only glance at the way that biblical scholarship gets caught up in the fads and preoccupations of the time. For instance, during the sixties there were innumerable volumes about Jesus and the poor, Jesus the revolutionary, and so forth. This means that anything we learn about the society at large will be true to a greater or lesser degree of our parishioners. The places we look to see what society is saying about itself are the media and the arts. We have already seen this about the arts in our references to Paul Tillich and Nathan Scott near the beginning of this chapter. Much of the validity of this reference to the media should be self-evident, but some aspects of it can be expanded in an illuminating way.

A runaway best-seller of the late fifties was Vance Packard's study of the use of depth psychology by advertisers, *The Hidden Persuaders.* Though much work has been done in the field since, this was the first introduction of most Americans to the way that they are manipulated by concealed appeals to their need for emotional security, for reassurance, for thinking well of themselves, for creativity that substitutes for child bearing and rearing, for something to love, for a sense of power that has sexual overtones, and for a hope of immortality to quiet one's fear of death. One implication of this revelation is that what advertisers say is not to be taken at its face value. This caution is necessary not only in detecting exaggerated claims but also in discovering the real as opposed to the surface motivation to which an appeal is being made. The power of an automobile engine, for instance, may be praised for providing "the extra margin of safety in an emergency," when what it is intended to offer a man is reassurance about his own virility. The psychiatrist in T.S. Eliot's play *The Cocktail Party*, Sir Henry Harcourt-Reilly, describes his work by saying,

I learn a good deal by merely observing you,
And letting you talk as long as you please,
And taking note of what you do not say.

The preacher needs to develop this capacity for taking note of what is not being said (though it is implied) not only in advertising, but in all else with which the media deal.

A recent cartoon in the *New Yorker* shows a newspaper kiosk on which are hanging magazines displaying the titles *Lust, Gluttony, Sloth, Greed, Pride, Anger,* and *Envy.* It would be an amusing party game to ask each person to draw up his own list of which magazine in his opinion panders most successfully to each of the seven deadly sins. That the *New Yorker* itself might deserve a place on the list is suggested by some of the ads from the same issue: We are told, for example, that one man shows that he really knows how to throw a party by never running out of a certain brand of Scotch. Wouldn't it be nice to be able to soothe all of our social insecurities just by purchasing that one brand of liquor? A silver punch bowl and its accessories are made virtuous by being described as a tribute to a great Englishman, Winston Churchill, at a time when inflation and the instability of the world money market are making anything in precious metal, however ridiculously molded, seem a desirable investment. Carriage lights that promise social prominence by their connection with the past and with vehicles touted as "the most elegant landaus and barouches" (Bet a quarter you can't describe either!) are offered by a Chicago department store that claims of itself, "There's nothing like it back home." Golfers are told that they can have clubs made that fit them as well as $400 suits, $100 shoes, or $30 ties. An automobile is promoted on the basis that it has qualities in common with seven other marques (one couldn't say brands) that cost at least twice as much. We receive the invaluable information that "when you're Spinnaker Riding in the Grenadines, an ill wind can bode you no good."

These ads are designed to appeal to people who might buy the products and are placed in magazines in which the advertisers expect them to be noticed by such people. Thus there is an inconsistency in the image of the readers held by the editors who select such cartoons and the advertisers who represent what the cartoon lampoons. The explanation for the inconsistency is probably not that either the editors or the advertisers are wrong but rather that the readership incorporates such inconsistencies. I know that I enjoy the cartoons that put down snobbism and yet at the same time would like to be able to afford some of the kinds of conspicuous consumption glorified in the ads. What the preacher needs to learn from all this is that he should listen to all of the things being said about our society in the media and not just those that are said explicitly in the articles, columns, and cartoons.

With this preface, we are now in position to see what the media actually have to tell us about the situations in which we find our people today. The obvious place to begin is with advertising since we have already introduced that topic. An advertisement is, among other things, a value statement. Some of them sound like counsels of despair. To be told that a particular brand of automobile is "something to believe in" or to be assured that "you only go round once in this life so you had better grab all the gusto you can get" and learn that the difference between the quality of the advertised brand and other cars or beers is the full range of achievement that is held out to us is to be reminded of the hopelessness of the materialistic view of life. He who would save his life will lose it indeed. The play made on our insecurities by TV commercials about bad breath, body odor, dirty dentures, etc. reveals to the one who would read the signs of the times the fears and anxieties about the most ordinary contacts of life which countless people have. Mrs. Olson and her mountain-grown coffee raise questions about the nature of the marriage relation in many homes. These are only a few of the more obvious indications of what we can learn about our society from its advertisements, and the reader can undoubtedly carry on his own list indefinitely.

The media to which a given preacher turns will depend a lot on his personal tastes and habits, but I have found that the newspapers remain my most plentiful sources for indications of what is occupying the attention of the people to whom I preach. A rough count of sources for sermons over a four-year period reveals newspapers in the lead. They come from all parts of the paper. News stories keep me informed on major current events and many of these cry out for analysis from a Christian point of view. It is hard to imagine, for instance, how a clergyman could have gone through the sixties without preaching on race relations, poverty, and Viet Nam, or more recently how he could have never got around to saying something from the pulpit about Watergate without being charged with culpable negligence. People need to understand the major issues of their time in a Christian perspective. This does not mean, of course, that the preacher's only or even major task is the denunciation of the sins of public figures who do not hear his sermons, but it does mean that people need help in fitting world events into their worldview. To become a Christian is to accept a Christian social construction of reality and to remain one requires that we continually legitimate that view by incorporating into it data which would appear to challenge it. Some of the things that have happened in recent years can be pretty threatening to a Christian worldview and the preacher has a duty to show how they can be fitted in.

Other news stories reveal things about our society. The fear of becoming involved that has permitted people to be murdered with no interference from people in the vicinity who could have helped is one example. Other stories, human interest stories, are ready-made parables just waiting for applications. Consider, for example, a story that broke in the Fall of 1972: a young mother, quite pretty to judge from the newspaper pictures, sick with a horrible disease, had two babies die and was told to have no more. She had no money to buy tombstones and so worked long hours to polish poured concrete gravemarkers for her two infants until they were as smooth as stone. A photograph revealed the markers to be neat, with careful and attractive lettering. Yet the city park board's cemetery committee said the headstones detracted from the appearance of the city's "showplace cemetery," so a follow-up story the next day showed her father helping her to remove the headstones. Shortly after she left for Germany to join her husband in the armed forces—defending the city fathers and their showplace cemetery.

Note that the point here is not that this story would make an excellent sermon illustration (although undoubtedly it would), but is rather that the story itself reveals something about our society and its values. At this point we are not concerned with how one constructs sermons, but with how he discovers the situations today that need preaching about. In this case, for instance, it would be an exercise in futility to castigate an absent council from another city, but the story may reveal to us something about our own concerns for appearance that override our responsiveness to human need. Other newspaper material that is also valuable can come from editorials, editorial cartoons, comic strips, syndicated columns, letters to the editor, feature stories, reviews of books, concerts, records, etc., investigative reports that are serialized through a week's issues, and so forth. It is very appropriate that a minister may deduct the cost of his newspaper as a business expense, because he could hardly do his job without one.

News magazines are also invaluable. The cover story on *Time* or *Newsweek* is one of the best indications of what issues are before the country that week. Another valuable feature is their parcelling out of the news into different departments, such as Art, Behavior, Books, etc. Regular attention to these keeps one from getting too specialized in his interests so that he neglects important trends in the culture. Yet the religious news in the news magazines is often one of the minister's best guides to spiritual trends in the society. It was through such sources that I learned of the growth of the teaching of Sri Aurobindo into a world religion, the Reverend Ike's gospel of wealth, a Japanese religion that promises spiritual development through golf, current statistics about the number of Roman Catholics who are leaving the priesthood, and *Newsweek*'s excellent cover story on Paul Moore, Episcopal Bishop of New York. Each of these told me something about the spiritual state of the society.

The possibilities offered by other kinds of magazines are as ubiquitous as the reading habits of clergy. The opportunities afforded by *Psychology Today, Esquire, Atlantic, Harper's, Playboy,* and *Fortune,* to name but a few, are immediately obvious. In fact, I believe that the only periodical that I have read with any frequency from which I have never gathered any sermon ideas is *Road & Track,* and maybe even there I just did not know how to interpret the data. Television, too, offers much to the regular viewer; one of its great advantages is that allusions to it have such a high degree of recognition by parishioners. This is an area in which I have little guidance to offer, since about all I watch is the *Today* show, news telecasts, documentaries, and movies that were not made for TV. The reason is not any sense of intellectual superiority, but is rather a sense of satiety, a sense of *deja vu ad nauseam*, to confuse tongues. I now find it hard to believe that I would find any situation comedy amusing or any TV thriller exciting. For anyone who is not burned out, however, the possibilities are many.

Something that I do pay a lot of attention to, though, is popular songs. I am not a rock fan; when my teen-age sons are playing records, I usually try to be in another part of the house. But when I drive any distance in the car I usually have the radio on and occasionally I hear lyrics that I find very arresting and quite illuminating. We are in a period (which may already be declining) when popular songs have content more serious than the moon/June/spoon sort of thing that I grew up on and are much more agreeable to listen to. Sometimes they have an explicit religious content; at other times the religious content is implicit, but none the less real for all that. "A Hard Rain's A-Gonna Fall" and "Eve of Destruction" are two songs that came from the mid-sixties, a period when the Church was secular enough in its orientation to be embarrassed about its traditional eschatological language, but when the counterculture was already beginning to use apocalyptic symbols. Other songs indicate the moral climate of the country in one way or another. Unless I badly misunderstand them, for instance, many love songs today praise the partner's skill in sexual intercourse. Certainly adultery is a major theme of the country music, which is becoming more widely accepted in our society. Whatever these trends show about changes in behavior patterns, they clearly show a change in permissible subjects and in attitudes. Here again I must emphasize that what we are talking about is listening to popular songs to hear what the congregation is saying about itself, not using lyrics to illustrate points based on other data. The illustrative use of lyrics is quite permissible and can be done brilliantly. One of the best sermons I ever heard, for example, was preached by the Rt. Rev. Albert R. Stuart and used the words to "Winchester Cathedral, You're Letting Me Down," to illustrate the secularity of the society that was being expressed in the "Death of God" theology. Often a song that reveals a situation may be used later to illuminate it, but we are still talking about recognizing the situation.

Movies are one of my favorite ways of listening to what the society is saying about itself. *Alice's Restaurant* once furnished me with a contemporary ideal of community life that allowed me to wrestle with the problem of what it means for a seminary to be a community. *Bonnie and Clyde, A Clockwork Orange,* and *M.A.S.H.* were all serious efforts at coming to grips with the violence of our society, while *The Godfather,* on the other hand, pandered to what Arthur Schlesinger, Jr. referred to as "the voyeurism of violence." *The Exorcist* manifests the contemporary preoccupation with the occult and, incidentally, has almost nothing in common with the New Testament understanding of demonic possession. *2001: A Space Odyssey,* though, is a beautifully theological interpretation of the history and future of technology. *Patton* was revelatory in the reaction it provoked, since it was praised equally by hawks who saw it as the portrait of a great hero and patriot, and doves who thought that it delineated clearly the psychopathy of the military mind. A society is in an interesting state when it can look at one artistic creation and come away with diametrically opposed interpretations.

Not a great deal needs to be said about film, since many parishes have become accustomed to using films to provoke theological discussion. We are advancing no new principle, but merely reiterating the familiar for the sake of completeness. A good book on the subject is *Seen Any Good Dirty Movies Lately?: A Christian Critic Looks at Contemporary Films* by James W. Arnold (who, incidentally, writes a regular column in the *Milwaukee Journal*).

Non-fiction books can be of significance in two ways: while on the one hand many of them intend to interpret contemporary culture, on the other the mere fact that some of them get written and published is itself quite revealing of the time in which we live. Skipping over obvious examples such as *The Joy of Sex*, we can think of the immense number of books that have come out in the last five years on ecology and American Indians. One of the first of the latter, *Custer Died for Your Sins*, was written by a son and grandson of Episcopal priests who were Sioux, Vine Deloria, Jr. His criticism of, among other things, Christianity as a missionary religion shows something about the success of the missionary movement. I once got the idea for a sermon from the religious listings in a publisher's list of new books since the books were overwhelmingly about non-Christian religions and often about spiritual masters from outside any of the major religious traditions. Thus we see that the mere fact that a book is published is itself an indication that there are enough people interested in its subject to make it likely that the book will be a commercial success. A bare list of books that are not explicitly religious out of which I have had sermons grow in the last few years is an indication of the range of possibilities:

Theodore Roszak, *The Making of a Counter Culture*
Paul Ehrlich, *The Population Bomb*
Alvin Toffler, *Future Shock*
Michael Harrington, *The Other America*
Haim Ginott, *Between Parent and Child*
Elisabeth Kübler-Ross, *On Death and Dying*
Dee Brown, *Bury My Heart at Wounded Knee*
Mike Royko, *Boss*
Daniel Boorstin, *The Image: A Guide to Pseudo-Events in America*

Here we reach a rather arbitrary line between the media and the arts. What we have to say about the arts as a source for understanding the situation in the pew will be seriously curtailed for several reasons. The first is that we have already given the theoretical basis for recognizing how the artist's understanding of society anticipates later developments, and we have also looked at Tillich's theory about the arts as material for theological reflection. Secondly, the manner in which many works of art are used by the preacher for his diagnosis of society is similar to that used for the media, which we have already examined. Finally, works of art for their very subtlety and complexity are not as co-optable for homiletical use as lesser works, even though they may contribute enormously to the preacher's personal insight.

The main thing that I have to say about most of the arts is a word of warning about the limitations on their use. None of these needs to be made about novels, but, since the theological interpretation of literature has now been made a theological discipline in its own right by Nathan A. Scott, Jr. and what now seems like an army of others, anything that could be said here would be manifestly superficial. Some of the novelists whom I have found most valuable in my preaching are Kazantzakis, Walker Percy, Graham Greene, and Kurt Vonnegut. I also have found crime fiction very useful but that is partly because I am an addict and thus only partly because as a pop art it is such a sensitive social barometer. Serious verse imposes such great demands on the listener that it seldom can be incorporated successfully into a sermon, as I discovered when I tried to use Yeats' "The Second Coming." Even though it often cannot be quoted, poetry can help the preacher know what to preach about. While Tillich's interpretation of Picasso's *Guernica* was a triumph and while I will never forget breakfast one morning with Allen Brockway, author of *The Secular Saint*, when we were graduate students, at which he gave an acute theological analysis of the painting of the fifties as an "art of uninvolvement," the preacher should never try to discuss a painting in a sermons without showing the congregation what it looks like. A whole academic specialty of the sociology of art is developing, however, that can alert the preacher to the social significance of painting and sculpture. References to drama are more effective if the congregation has had an opportunity to see the play. In all of these warnings I have assumed that the work of art in question will be used not only to apprise the preacher of the situation in the pew, but will be used also by him to make those in the pew aware of their own position.

At the end of such a long list of tools, a reminder of what they are to be used for is in order. The preacher discovers from his exegesis what the situation in the text is that is to be related to the life of the Church today. Next the preacher draws on his knowledge of the many situations in the congregation that his contacts with the congregation and his exposure to the media and the arts have given him to select the single situation in the congregation that most nearly matches the template of the situation in that day's text.

How to Bring the Two
Together in a Sermon

So far we have discussed how we discover the two main
ingredients of a sermon, the situation in the text and the
situation in the pew, but we have not yet dealt with how
these are fitted together to make a sermon. What we have
at this point is just the raw materials, not the finished
product. There is a classic and traditional manner for
beginning a sermon with which we are all familiar. The
minister announces his text and then begins to expound it,
making clear what it was intended to mean to its first
readers. Then and only then does he move on to apply it
to the lives of the congregation. In a way, this seems
logical enough because it is the order in which the
preacher went about preparing his sermon, but the order
of preparation is not necessarily the order of presentation.
Beginning with the text presupposes something that is
unfortunately unlikely to be true: that contemporary
Christians have a great deal of interest in the Bible itself
and a lot of curiosity about solving the riddles posed by its
interpretation. That may have been true of Christians at
various times in history. It has been said that Scottish

congregations stay awake for the first five minutes of a sermon to make certain that the minister's exegesis and theology are sound and then, knowing that they are secure, fall asleep. In the near-Fundamentalist circles in which I was a boy, the announcement of a familiar text by a new preacher excited a lot of interest in how he would interpret it, much as dramatic audiences might wish to see how an actor performs Hamlet or concertgoers will see how a conductor reads Beethoven. An audience of connoisseurs enjoys judging a virtuoso performance. Modern congregations, however, seldom have familiarity with the biblical texts themselves, much less with the various ways in which they have been treated in the past. They lack the background and the peer group to go in for the sort of sermon-tasting that we have been describing. For that reason, when a preacher begins by announcing a text, he loses most of his audience instantly.

A much sounder method of beginning a sermon is suggested by Winnie-the-Pooh:

Sometimes Winnie-the-Pooh likes a game of some sort when he comes downstairs, and sometimes he likes to sit quietly in front of the fire and listen to a story. This evening—

"What about a story?" said Christopher Robin.

"*What* about a story?" I said.

"Could you very sweetly tell Winnie-the-Pooh one?"

"I suppose I could," I said. "What sort of stories does he like?"

"About himself. Because he's *that* sort of Bear." [1]

This is not to say that people are egocentric (although that is one way of expressing what we mean by original sin), but is rather to say that most people are more interested in life today than they are in life two to four thousand years ago. Even if they consider the events of the biblical past to be revelatory, they expect the revelation to have some relevance to their lives. They expect it to reveal something about their situation. Thus the place to begin is where they are.

This has been recognized for at least half a century now. The first publication of this theory that I know anything about was an article by Harry Emerson Fosdick entitled "What Is the Matter with Preaching?" that appeared in *Harper's Magazine* for July, 1928. The correction that he offered for the ills of the sermon was:

Start with a life issue, a real problem, personal or social, perplexing the mind or disturbing the conscience; face the problem fairly, deal with it honestly, and throw some light on it from the spirit of Christ, that people will be able to go out able to think more clearly and live more nobly because of that sermon.[2]

Halford E. Luccock has demonstrated successfully how much Fosdick's insight was derived from the pedagogical revolution that was going on at the time. Until near the time that Fosdick wrote, the approved method of teaching was that commended by the German philosopher and pedagogical theoretician, Johann Friedrich Herbart. He said that good teaching began by preparing the mind for the new subject matter, presenting it, showing its relation to knowledge or ideas already familiar, drawing generalizations or conclusions on the basis of it, and then discovering applications of it. John Dewey, however, had recently been convincing educators that the proper order of learning was:

1. A felt difficulty.
2. Location and definition of the difficulty.
3. Suggestion of possible solutions.
4. Development by reasoning of bearings of suggestions.
5. Further observation and exploration leading to acceptance or rejection of the solution.

This problem-solving approach to preaching advocated by

Fosdick made it possible to start with people where they were in order to get them where one wanted them to go.[3]

A much more sophisticated treatment of the whole issue has been given by Clement W. Welsh in a book that carries the title *Preaching in a New Key*, but which has the much more informative subtitle, *Studies in the Psychology of Thinking and Learning*. Episcopal clergy who have gone to the College of Preachers at the National Cathedral in Washington for post-ordination training during the last decade have become very accustomed to the distinction that Welsh, who is Warden there, makes between "kerygmatic" and "pre-kerygmatic" preaching. This distinction, which he borrowed from the Jesuit missionary to Japan, Alphonse Nebreda, recognizes that because of one kind of cultural impediment or another, many people are incapable of hearing the gospel when it is proclaimed in straightforward kerygmatic preaching. There must be a preparation for the gospel that starts with the experience that people already have and the world they already know and builds from that to the gospel; this preparation is what is designated as pre-kerygmatic preaching. Welsh takes this initial insight from Nebreda and carries it a good bit further by recognizing that in order to start with people where they are, one must have some real understanding of the process of how people not merely learn, but actually change their basic stance toward life.

He meets the need for this sort of understanding on the part of the preacher by writing a book that only gets around to developing a strategy for preaching in the last couple of chapters. Rather than a collection of helpful practical hints on sermon writing like this book, Welsh's book focuses on the audience of the sermon and uses the insights of modern communication theory to show the preacher how people understand and accept ideas so that he can tailor his sermons to accomplish that goal. Preaching, Welsh says, attempts to get people thinking seriously about making sense of the universe and their place in it. While this kind of fundamental thinking comes to all of us with difficulty, it is necessary to the human psyche and is actually initiated at a very early age by all of us. Because this sense of what the world is like is so basic to our stability, it is the most difficult kind of thinking to change, hence the tremendous challenge of the preacher's task. Indeed, the people whom we would like most to change are those who are most "rigid," "concrete," or "closed" in their thinking. This is to say that they are the people who are most threatened by new ideas and who are best prepared to defend against them. In the light of this understanding, then, Welsh gives in the closing lines of his book his understanding of the preacher's task:

We preach to primitive men and women (in the sense that they are concerned with their "primitive" or "central" beliefs about the universe, human nature, themselves, and reality), for whom the rote acceptance of great answers can bring no relief until the great questions have been asked. Set within the framework of the liturgy, surrounded by the Word, secure within the community of trust, guided by the man of faith, the sermon event may be rediscovered as an event in which the people of this fragile planet may begin to understand how meanings may be found, and may begin to see themselves as the people of God.[4]

It is obvious that Welsh urges the preacher to begin with the congregation not only in the outline of the sermon, but also in the way that he conceives the whole structure of it. Instead of saying that what the preacher starts with is a life situation, he refers to it as "the creation," which is the only thing that is "common to us all, to all cultures and to all degrees of religious interest within a culture."[5] But this more ontological way of stating things does not exclude, I think, a view of the universe that makes references to the creation, and at the same time references to the existential experience of what it means to live in the universe. Welsh compares the preacher's way of dealing with creation to that of the dramatist.

A play . . . selects a portion of the creation and unfolds it, working hard to maintain accuracy in its development of the bit of reality chosen, and to excite the audience to perceive more and more the meaning of it." [6]

Sermons, too, start with "a luminous piece of reality." They focus the attention of the audience on that reality for a controlled period of time, as plays do, and with both media there is "the freedom of the listener to discover meaning for himself, and the stimulation of the listener's imagination to find deeper and deeper levels of significance." [7] Sermons that are written with this concept in mind and that strive to achieve their impact not by a tightly reasoned argument, but by leading the listener to respond to the particular bit of reality held up for examination, are not as threatening to "primitive" thinking as arguments are. They offer the hearer a chance to change by providing the opportunity to respond directly to the data of creation itself and not to conclusions drawn from that data. Thus such pre-kerygmatic sermons are keyed much more directly to knowledge of how thought changes than kerygmatic sermons are, and can, therefore, lead people who are closed in their thinking to become open to new insights about the meaning of the universe.

The insight that preaching should begin with the situation of the hearer is by no means as new as the twentieth century. Jesus himself did this in his preaching. It is a commonplace that Jesus' favorite pedagogical technique was the use of parables, but the importance of this is often missed by people who think of parables as illustrations of points that Jesus was trying to make and fail to recognize that they fuction as arguments as well. For over a generation now scholars have recognized that what Jesus taught in parables and by other means was that in his ministry the reign of God was breaking into history. Most of his preaching was addressed to the unconverted and often to the antagonistic. Jesus used the parable to try to convince these opponents that the kingdom of God was about to be inaugurated. It has been the contribution of Eta Linnemann, a German New Testament scholar who was trained in the New Hermeneutic, to show how these parables functioned as arguments.

In the parables Jesus offers his opponents an analogy to the situation about which he is preaching. It has to be an analogy that they will accept as valid and, in order for them do so, Jesus makes a concession to their point of view. The parable, after conceding a certain limited validity to the position of Jesus' opponents, goes on to invite them to look at the same situation from a different perspective. In the Prodigal Son, for instance, there is an initial concession that the boy got what he deserved, but then the hearer is asked to look at the matter from an entirely different angle, that of the father of the young man, who was far more interested in having his son than he was in seeing the wages of sin paid off. By his initial concession, Linnemann says that Jesus "interlocked" the point of view of his opponents with his own so that they were compelled then to consider the new point of view that he offered them in the story. And when they had seen that new point of view, they had to make a decision about it. They could no longer ignore it. They could either accept it or reject it, knowing all that could be said for what they rejected and taking full responsibility for their decision.

As Linnemann says, "the relevant feature in the parable evokes the same or at least a similar attitude as the listeners have taken to the reality in question." [8] There are many similarities to the parables used by Jesus as arguments and what we have said in the first two chapters about sermons. Jesus calls attention to a situation in the life of the audience. He brings forward another situation, which he presents as analogous to the first. In the case of the teaching of Jesus, the analogy is the parable, but in the case of the sermon, it is the situation in the text that we claim shares a common principle with the life situation. When the analogy is granted as valid, the attitude in the parable or biblical story is transferred to the situation of the hearer, and it is recognized that the transfer is legitimate.

This, then, is the way that the situation in the text and the situation in the pew are brought together in the sermon. The sermon outline consists of three steps to make one point. The first step is that the situation in the congregation is depicted, the second is that the situation in the Bible is shown to be analogous, and the third is that the attitude toward the situation in the text is transferred to the contemporary situation. Some things need to be said about each of these steps.

There are two points that need to be made about the first step. The first is that the life situation may be a matter of either "central" or "intermediate" belief, as these terms are used by Welsh after Rokeach. That is to say that the sermon may deal with either an ultimate question about the meaning of life or with a less global but nevertheless real question about authority, what people are like, and thus what norms of behavior are. The "preaching in a new key" that Welsh calls for would deal with such central questions; these may also be recognized as the existential questions that Tillich says call for the answer of revelation. Most of the life situations that Fosdick spoke of are, on the other hand, questions of intermediate beliefs. A sermon, as we said, may deal with either kind. The second point to be made about the life situation is that we are alerted to it by our exposure to our parishioners, to the media, and to the arts, and whatever in those sources it was that alerted us to that situation may be (although it is not necessarily) "the luminous piece of reality" spoken of by Welsh. And it is that "piece of reality" that we use in the sermon itself to lead our hearers into a consideration of the life situation. In the last chapter there was some confusion when congregational contacts, media, and arts were discussed as indications of the situations our people are in, because it is also possible to employ those same data in the sermon to document the situation we wish to consider. At this point I must warn against thinking of these data as illustrations. They participate in the reality they depict, so they are not merely similar to it. Welsh states the point with great accuracy:

Ordinarily, an abstract idea is brought home to the congregation by an illustration from human experience; idea is primary, illustration is secondary. In pre-kerygmatic preaching the illustration *is* the sermon; the illustration, extended and given a dramatic life of its own, is primary, and the ideas generated by it are secondary.[9]

In regard to step two, the demonstration of the analogy between the situation in the congregation and that in the biblical text, the main point that needs to be made is that the amount of exegesis that gets into the sermon is only the amount that is necessary to make it possible for the congregation to understand what the text is about. On the whole the sermon should incorporate the results of exegesis and not its apparatus. There are occasions, such as sermons at theological seminaries, on which one might expect a certain amount of curiosity about biblical scholarship in its own right, but otherwise most of the steps that the preacher goes through in arriving at his own understanding of the passage should not become a part of his public presentation. When, however, the congregation will not see how he derived his point from the text without being shown the method employed, enough must be reported to indicate that the procedure was legitimate and the conclusions sound. Instead of an elaborate demonstration of the preacher's erudition, what is called for is a vivid reconstruction of the human situation that the text grows out of, a reconstruction whose features in common with the modern situation are clearly marked. As we said, the purpose of this step is to demonstrate the analogy between the two situations.

The purpose of the third step is the purpose of the whole sermon: to help the hearer arrive at insight into the situation in his own life or the life of the community at a parochial or larger level that he had his original question about. In some sermons, especially those that deal with central questions, the attitude that is transferred from the biblical situation to his own situation will be simply a perspective in which to view the situation. This kind of sermon is attitude-forming and the attitudes involved are the basic ones that a person needs to make sense of the universe. In other sermons that deal with intermediate matters, what might be transferred is a principle by which one decides upon a proper course of action. Some sermons, indeed, will end properly with an exhortation to do a particular thing. All sermons will expect some direct response from the congregation, even if that response is only to alter an attitude. In fact, with the ultimateness of some of the attitudes at stake, the most important responses to sermons will be at that level.

An additional point about the construction of the sermon that needs to be made and yet does not fit in with anything else said can be inserted here as conveniently as anywhere else. It has to do with the language in which the sermon is couched. In the past the language of the sermon has usually been elevated discourse, probably on the assumption that serious matters should be discussed gravely. This has meant that sermons have been formal and at times even stilted. The rhetorical embellishments have been of the sort we call oratorical. Striking uses of language, arresting phrases, and poetical flourishes have been expected at times. This is not the appropriate diction for the sort of sermon we have been considering. Instead, the language should be conversational. It may be slangy at times and even deliberately provocative. There are several reasons why this is so. The first is that oratory is no longer in fashion and so people have a reflexive tendency to distrust it. Then, too, there is a tendency in elevated discourse to talk down, which is inappropriate to the gospel. Probably the most important reason, though, is a matter of what McLuhan would describe as the relation of the medium to the message. The technique of this sort of preaching is not to tell the congregation what they should think so much as to lead them through a process by which they will discover for themselves what they should think. The kind of language that is appropriate, then, is the sort that a person uses in thinking to himself. In other words, it is the most intimate, direct, and relaxed sort of language possible.

Because of this desire to lead the congregation to insight, one might occasionally think that even the three-step, one-point pattern for the sermon that we have outlined above is too directive. At such times I have employed a different outline that called upon the congregation for even more participation—changing the sermon from a "hot" to a "cool" medium, to use McLuhan's terminology. The method, to the best of my knowledge, was derived ultimately from Kierkegaard and proximately from my colleague on the faculty at Nashotah House, Robert Cooper. It would receive approval, I believe, from Welsh, who wrote in a recent *College of Preachers Newsletter* of the preacher as midwife, using the Platonic metaphor for describing one who assists "the listener to bring to birth ideas already present in his mind."[10] This pattern (to the extent that it can be called one) is what I call a "Do-It-Yourself" sermon. It consists of presenting several "exhibits" along with the biblical text or some aspect of it. They are chosen because they appear to have something in common with the situation in the text, some common principle operating between them—if you do not assume that by "principle" I mean some abstract statement that can be extrapolated from them and then regarded as their "meaning." These exhibits are presented straight, with no interpretation and no effort to interrelate them. Sometimes they consist of articles from the newspaper, read as they were written or with judicious pruning. At other times an event that I remember or have heard of will be used. At still others a novel or poem will furnish the material. The interrelation and the drawing of insight are left entirely up to the congregation.

I believe that I have never used the method myself when discussion was not to follow, but I think that it could be done that way, especially if the people were told what to expect. When discussion has followed, I have been impressed with the quality of it. People seem to perceive meaning better without direction than they do with it, if one may judge from these experiences. The method should be used with caution and with economy, but with those strictures in mind, it can be recommended as a very effective way of getting the situation in the pew together with the situation in the text.

How to Deliver the Sermon
So That It Will Be Heard

An experience that anyone who has preached for very long is bound to have had is that of being told by someone that a certain sermon helped him a great deal at a critical time in his life. The flattered preacher asks what particular point was so helpful and is flabbergasted to be told something that he does not recall saying. This experience points to something that should have been obvious all along, but seldom gets noticed: The content of the sermon is not just what the preacher said, but includes what was heard by all of those present. Each individual comes to a sermon with a pre-understanding that is the result of all his previous efforts to make sense of life. These efforts, in turn, are based on the sum total of all that person's experiences. This means that the hearer will try to fit what the preacher says with what he knows already. In some cases he will lack the experience to discover anything recognizable in the sermon and so will be unable to attach it to anything he already knows. At other times (and these happen more often than we would like to think), members of the congregation have more extensive experience than the minister and they can verify or correct all that was said. Most frequently of all, though, the experience of the audience will just be different and the differences will add color and nuance to the way they hear the sermon.

Another factor that determines what parishioners hear in a sermon is their own immediate experience, especially the concerns that have been occupying their attention. This will furnish the context in which they hear and apply the things that are said in the sermon and thus give an entirely different shape to the sermon. I remember having a woman ask once, "Did you mean such and such?" The only reply that I could honestly give was, "No, I did not mean that because I was not smart enough to think of it. If I had been, though, that is what I would have meant!"

Now if the content of the sermon is not just what the preacher says, but includes all that the congregation hears, provision should be made for making that additional content explicit. In other words, a sermon should be followed by discussion whenever possible. There are a number of reasons why this is so. The first is that it furnishes the minister with the best possible sort of feedback so that he can know if he is being understood. All too often, all the preacher is told about his sermons is what people tell him as he greets them at the church door after the service. The data that is accumulated there is something that clergy have never really known how to deal with. What is said is usually complimentary and many preachers try to steel themselves against having their egos bloated by this praise. Yet the praise itself is often almost ritual in its fixed and conventional formulae and other clergy feel that God's Word and they themselves have somehow been demeaned by being told that a sermon was "nice." My own guess is that both reactions are overreactions to an expression of the good intentions and will of well-bred people. Eric Berne would say that the preacher is receiving the appropriate number of strokes and that the transaction should not be interpreted beyond that for additional semantic content. The point is that the clergyman does need some accurate feedback so that he knows how effectively he is communicating, and discussion of what he has said is one of the best ways of letting him know if he has been understood.

The next reason why there should be discussion is that it makes preaching responsible. This is true in the obvious and literal sense that the sermon will expect a response. But it is also true in the deeper sense that the preacher will be held accountable for what he says. A clergyman told me that his whole preaching style changed as a result of conducting services in a prison on a regular basis during one period of his ministry. Not only could the inmates vote with their feet by not returning, they would also say during the sermon what they thought of what was being said, and their opinions were not always complimentary nor was their language always polite. He discovered then that he had to be willing to stand by what he said and to stand or fall with it. Some clergy may be afraid of learning what people think of their preaching and they are the ones who most need to know. To be willing to speak in the name of the Lord is an awesome responsibility; indeed a man takes a great deal upon himself when he presumes to occupy the attention of a number of people for stated times at regular intervals. He should have to answer for it.

Discussion also makes preaching responsible in the obligation it places upon the congregation to take the sermon seriously. Many lay people may get the idea for the first time that the sermon is supposed to be about something and that it is meant to be listened to. For many people, the introductory formulae for sermons have always been understood as cues to begin periods of free association, wool-gathering, and fantasy. The knowledge that they are to discuss the sermon later could be a powerful incentive to listen to it.

Another argument for discussion of sermons is that it commits the congregation more deeply to what is said. A vestryman once suggested to me (and not entirely facetiously) that we should have a sign erected that said, "The opinions expressed in this pulpit do not necessarily reflect those of the vestry." It is possible for a congregation or members of it to assume an adversary relation to the preacher, taking the position that what he says is his affair and of no necessary significance to them. When they have discussed the sermon, though, and argued their own way to the conclusions, they are bound by the conclusions of their own thought process. The implications of the sermon are no longer just a matter of the minister's opinion, but are instead one's own totalling of the evidence in a way that makes one responsible for the implications of the answer.

The most important reason for discussion, though, is that the clergyman is not the only person with spiritual insight. Another way of saying the same thing is that he does not have an exclusive pipeline to heaven. The Holy Spirit can speak through the unordained as well as the ordained. We have seen already that the content of the sermon is not just what the minister said, but also what every member of the congregation heard. The insights that the parishioners have are valuable and should be shared. I have had occasions on which my sermon "bombed out" completely, sermons that no one could get into deeply enough to discuss. I have been fortunate, though, that when it became obvious that no one was going to discuss the sermon, someone asked a question about which he had been wondering. Apparently other people were bothered by the same thing, because these questions prompted better discussion than the sermon would have.

Although provision for discussion after a sermon is a relatively recent thing, the idea of making provision for including the point of view of the congregation in a sermon is not new. Although today we are inclined to think of Cynics as "people who know the price of everything and the value of nothing," in the ancient world they were a school of itinerant philosophers and moralists who resembled a cross between primitive Franciscans and the more serious hippies. They developed a very effective form of popular preaching called the diatribe, which was not, as it is today, a bitter and abusive verbal attack, but an informal sort of address that had the feel of dialogue because it would state the supposed opinion of the audience and then respond to that. The style became very influential and is even detectable several places in the New Testament, especially in some of the letters of St. Paul.

More recently, however, we have seen efforts to represent different points of view by different voices so that two or more persons would speak from the chancel. At times both who spoke were clergy although one voiced the opinions of the man in the pew while the other responded to them. At other times real representatives of other points of view would speak their own opinions. A popular series of such sermons that was preached at the Cathedral of St. John the Divine in New York had a member of the congregation speak as a troubled soul while James A. Pike and Howard A. Johnson, at that time Dean and Canon Theologian of the cathedral, spoke as a "Tempter" and a "Voice." While this sort of thing was very popular about twenty years ago, I have not heard much of it recently and I believe that it has almost disappeared. My guess about the reason it has done so is that, for all its sound intentions, it must have seemed gimmicky and contrived. Other methods have been tried for giving the congregation input into the sermon. Some clergy have sermon-planning sessions with representatives of the congregation, who discuss with them both the biblical passages to be interpreted and contemporary issues on which sermons are thought desirable. In other parishes designated individuals meet to evaluate a sermon after it has been preached. Both practices can be very useful.

The kind of sermon that is spoken through several voices is called a "dialogue sermon." That term is also used by some to refer to sermons followed by discussion. The two have been distinguished by William D. Thompson and Gordon C. Bennett as *chancel dialogue* and *congregational dialogue*. It seems to me that the difference between the two is more important than any common features they may share because the one has someone speak for the members of the congregation while the other allows the congregation to speak for itself. Some churches that have tried congregational dialogue have begun the discussion after the minister only read the scripture lesson and indicated in a few remarks what biblical scholars said about the original meaning of the passage with no effort to interpret or apply the passage today. Rather, the purpose of the discussion was to make that application.

I think that there are major disadvantages to that procedure. The first is that discussion usually proceeds better when it is a little more focused than that, when it is on a particular topic on which people have already been thinking rather than consisting of spur-of-the-moment reactions. The other is that the clergyman is both the member of the congregation who has been set apart to proclaim the gospel and to speak authoritatively in the name of the Church, and he is also the member who has undergone professional training in biblical interpretation, theology, and morals. Thus it is likely that the best discussion will follow sermons that have been prepared by him to prompt such discussion. In the previous chapter we said that the language of a sermon should at times be deliberately provocative. What the language should provoke is constructive discussion after the sermon.

Such discussion poses immense difficulties of logistics

and there is no solution that will be serviceable in every situation and probably none that will be perfect in any. For instance, the classic occasion for the delivery of a sermon is the regular Sunday morning service in the church. It is very hard to have discussion in that context because of time and also because many people find it difficult to speak out in church. It seems to them somehow irreverent. On the other hand, when a sermon is preached at the liturgy and is discussed at an adult class or coffee hour that follows, the immediacy has been lost and much of the impact of the sermon is forgotten and gone. It is hard to recapture the mood and to get the discussion off the ground. The method that I have found to be most satisfactory in the places that I have tried it is to omit the sermon from the service in church entirely, having at most a short homily directed mainly at the children there, and then when everyone is comfortably settled in the parish house with a cup of coffee and a sweetroll or cigarette, preach a formal sermon of ten to fifteen minutes in length that is followed by two to three times that much time devoted to discussion. This way the people are relaxed and ready to give themselves to the consideration of the subject, they have the sermon fresh in their minds, they feel no inhibitions about saying their mind, and they have time to do so.

The main reservation I have had about this procedure has been liturgical and theological. I think the sermon should be a part of the liturgy. I am not sure that I have really found an answer to this objection, but I do have a rationalization that I am willing to live with. It has happened (and I am grateful that it has) that the services at which I have preached regularly during the time I was developing this method of preaching were family eucharists. In the primitive Church the Eucharist was held in the context of a meal. Later the sacrament was separated from the meal and came to be regarded as a cultic act while the meal was an occasion of fellowship within the body. My rationalization is that the coffee hour is the modern equivalent of the *agape* fellowship meal and shares in the eucharistic context. Thus the sermon remains in the liturgical bracketing that it had in the primitive Church. I do not know how far I would want to push that, but I do know that on the other hand I would be very suspicious of the theology of anyone who would pose too radical a distinction and separation between what is done in the church as liturgy and what is done in the parish house as fellowship.

Much more needs to be said about leading the discussion than can be said here. For this expertise the minister will have to call upon group skills that he has acquired elsewhere. If he has not had such training he should get it anyway, quite apart from its usefulness here. I must content myself with a few very general remarks based on experience. The first is that it takes people a little while to get themselves collected and ready to start talking after the sermon is over. It is easy for the minister to be intimidated by the silence and to begin discussing his sermon himself. That is the surest possible way to keep the congregation from ever discussing it. The technique is to wait them out. I usually use this time to get a cup of coffee myself. Eventually the silence will make the congregation nervous and someone will say something just to break the silence. That starts the ball rolling and you usually have no trouble after that.

Another pitfall, and one that I fall into all too readily, is the tendency to have a question and answer session rather than a discussion. The preacher becomes the authority figure who has the answers. Thus the time that should have been spent on the contributions of the people is usurped to give the professional mouth more platform time. I am not convinced that the minister should become merely a moderator who has nothing to contribute to the discussion, but I do think that he should not monopolize it. He does want to be careful to recognize each person who wishes to be heard and he must try to make each speaker feel that his contribution has been recognized. It will inevitably happen that someone will say something that does not appear to advance the topic. The moderator can then attempt a short paraphrase of what was said and ask for other contributions. In this way he can keep the speaker from feeling neglected and yet not allow the discussion to die. There will, of course, be the more verbal members of the group who will want to speak often. There will be times when discussion is slow and you will be grateful for them, especially if they really have something to say—as they often do. When others who seldom speak are trying to do so, though, the more aggressive speakers will have to be held in check politely but firmly. Occasionally the moderator can helpfully serve as a process reporter, helping the group keep straight on the progress of the discussion or reflecting to them his feelings about the way things are going. Undoubtedly a hundred hints more helpful than these will occur to the reader, who is likely to know that a good discussion is seldom achieved accidentally.

This concludes the presentation of the method of biblical preaching that I propose. Now follows the illustration of it. Before we move on to that it might be useful just to repeat what the four steps are in this one method of preaching from the Bible today:

1. Exegete the biblical passage to be preached from so that you understand thoroughly the situation it was originally addressed to and the attitude the writer takes toward that situation.

2. Drawing on your contacts with your people in visiting, counselling, and hearing confessions, and your exposure to the media and the arts, select the situation in

the life of the congregation that most closely resembles the situation in the biblical text.

3. Compose a sermon that begins by inviting the congregation to reflect on their own situation and then moves on to show that the situation in the text is analogous, and concludes by applying to the situation in the congregation the attitude taken in the text toward the situation there.

4. Deliver the sermon in a setting where it can be followed by congregational discussion that will take two or three times as long as the sermon itself did.

PART II

Examples

A Sermon to Preachers

Thursday after 15th Trinity, 1971
Nashotah House
First Lesson, Evening Prayer*

This sermon is not an example of the method so much as it is a justification for it, being a sermon that was preached to seminarians; it is more technically exegetical than a parochial sermon would be and uses the way the evangelists themselves handle the gospel tradition to argue for a way of approaching the Bible homiletically today. Thus this sermon is addressed to the reader of this book in a way that those that follow are not.

Tonight for the first time I am glad that the Senior class is so small. I do not mean that I'm glad that there are no more like them; we could do with lots more. My pleasure is rather in the fact that so small a portion of the congregation has taken my course in synoptics, because anyone who has taken that course could write my sermon for me. They know what I am going to say. As soon as the lector began reading the second lesson and they heard

---

* The first page of all my sermon manuscripts contains the date and place of the sermon and the biblical text for it.

Matthew's account of the stilling of the storm, the cat was out of the bag.

You see, one of the most brilliant pieces of modern exegesis is an article by Günther Bornkamm on this passage. This article is, in fact, one of the initial experiments in Redaction Criticism which demonstrated the utility of this tool for understanding the gospels. The Seniors know, then, that I cannot preach on this pericope without using the article of Bornkamm that I forced them to read as an example of how gospel exegesis ought to be done. Thus they have my permission to turn off their hearing aids now and go to sleep. But the rest of you had better sit up and take notice. It might be useful later.

As Mark told it, the stilling of the storm is a straightforward miracle story, characterized by great vividness and realism. Jesus is seen as the one who has power over even the demonic forces of chaos represented in a storm at sea. The whole story turns on the contrast between the condition of the weather before and after Jesus spoke his word of power.

That element is still strong in Matthew, but under the evangelist's skillful hand the story takes on another dimension as well. Without ponderous allegory, the stilling of the storm becomes a description of the situation of the Church in Matthew's day. The Church is the boat, tossed about in a hostile world. The Christians of Matthew's Church have their counterpart in the disciples in the boat. They, too, in the face of the danger that confronts them, display little faith. Yet, if in that faith they turn to the Lord, he will help them and save them from the dangers that threaten.

The work of Matthew is so facile that it takes a gifted exegete to discover it. The first clue that Bornkamm notes is that the story is set by Matthew in a context in which discipleship is being discussed. It is the chapter after the Sermon on the Mount, that great treatise on the subject of discipleship, and it comes in a series of stories that illustrate what discipleship means. A man tells Jesus that he wants to follow him wherever he goes, but Jesus says that he is not so fortunate as a fox or a bird in having a home. Another man says that he must bury his father, but Jesus says, "Follow me and let the dead bury their dead." The key word in these stories is *follow*; discipleship means following. Immediately after these incidents about following, Jesus and his disciples go on board the boat. Matthew says: "Jesus got into the boat and his disciples followed him." In Mark the whole thing is quite different: Jesus was already on the boat preaching from its prow and it sailed when the disciples came aboard. Matthew has altered this so that he can join this story to the two preceding ones by the catchword *follow*, thus telling us that its meaning is to be understood in the light of theirs. This story too is about discipleship.

With this working hypothesis, Bornkamm notes several other features of Matthew's re-telling of the stilling of the storm which support the interpretation. One is the title by which Jesus is addressed. In Mark Jesus is called simply Teacher, Rabbi. In Luke he is called by another term of human respect, Master. But in Matthew the disciples turn in their fear to the one they address as *kyrie*, Lord. Their cry is virtually a *kyrie eleison*. We could be making too much of this; at times *kyrie* means no more than 'Sir,' but Bornkamm shows that the word when used by Matthew is a divine predicate of majesty. It is the Church's exalted Lord whom the disciples call upon in their distress.

Another difference between the way that Matthew tells the story and the other evangelists do is that they have Jesus rebuke the disciples for their lack of faith after he has quieted the storm, but in Matthew he rebukes their little faith before they have seen this display of his mighty power. The disciples in Matthew's Church show a lack of faith before they have seen the hand of the Lord at work.

But their little faith is not an absence of faith; it is rather that kind of faith, Matthew is telling them, that has power to move mountains. They should not become discouraged if their faith is not stronger. Even the apostles themselves had only little faith, but when in that little faith they turned to their Lord in prayer, he was able to deliver them. He can do the same for the members of Matthew's Church.

It is on the basis of this evidence and some other that Bornkamm is able to say:

Matthew is not only a hander-on of the narrative, but is also its oldest exegete, and in fact the first to interpret the journey of the disciples with Jesus in the storm with reference to disciple-ship, and that means with reference to the little ship of the Church.[1]

It could be very profitable for us to apply this to our own situation, to ask what it means for us to be disciples of Jesus in the storm-tossed world of today, but since Tuesday was the feast of St. Matthew, I think that we might treat this passage as an example of the saintliness of Matthew, as a model for us to imitate. Luckily, Dave Olson preached about Matthew the Apostle, so I can say something about Matthew the Evangelist without being redundant.

Bornkamm has spoken of Matthew as both a hander-on and an exegete of tradition about Jesus. As priests you will also be called upon to interpret the tradition about Jesus and apply it to the lives of your people. Seeing how Matthew went about his job can tell us something about how we ought to do ours.

The first thing we notice is that when Matthew wanted to help his congregation to understand their situation, it was to the tradition about Jesus that he turned. God spoke his fullest word about himself to man in the life of Jesus and all we know about God and his will for his world is what we learn by reflecting on the accounts of that life that have come down to us. We are the people who have accepted this norm for our understanding of reality. We have accepted it, of course, because in it we have acquired the vocabulary for understanding and communicating our own deepest experiences of reality. One way of defining the Church is to call it the body of people who understand reality in terms of the revelation of Jesus. Just as Matthew called upon the tradition about Jesus to illuminate the situation of his congregation, we will have to call upon it for our own efforts to help our people to understand their situation. To state it baldly and controversially, I think that ordinarily sermons should be based on the gospel for the day.

The next thing we notice about Matthew's work as a transmitter of tradition about Jesus is that he was not content just to transmit. As Bornkamm puts it, he both handed on and he exegeted the tradition. He applied the tradition to the situation of his congregation. The word about Jesus is not gospel for us as long as it remains merely a word about the past; it must be also a word about the present to speak to us. As Matthew told us, "Every teacher of the law who becomes a disciple in the kingdom of heaven is like a homeowner who takes new and old things out of his storage room" (13:15).

To be controversial again, if not downright provocative, one of the things that worries me about the Jesus People is their persistence in using the same vocabulary to describe all situations. This, however, is not just a matter of repeating the tradition about Jesus without interpreting it; it is not the old that is brought out of their storage rooms but the new, since the categories into which they try to squeeze all experience are not so much those of the gospels as they are those of nineteenth-century Revivalism, which they have imposed on the gospel. To make the gospel real to your people, you will have both to state it in language they understand and also to show them how it makes their own lives not only understandable but even capable of redemption.

The third thing we notice about Matthew's use of the tradition about Jesus is that he applied it to the lives of his people by the best methods of interpretation available to him at the time. He was himself the teacher of the Law who became a disciple of the kingdom of Heaven. Indeed, Krister Stendahl has suggested that Matthew's gospel is the product of a school of Christian rabbis. This theory is based mainly on the fact that Matthew has a number of Old Testament proof texts that are not quoted by the other evangelists as predictions of Christ, but it could also be supported by this midrashic use of tradition about Jesus that we see in tonight's second lesson.

But the methods of interpretation that were best for Matthew are not the best methods for us. The high demands of interpretation of scripture have been stated by Quentin Quesnell in an article he wrote about Bernard Lonergan. The scriptures have to be understood, he says, as "talking about reality." That means that they have to be applied in the "best possible senses,"

senses conformable to the ultimate standards of truth, the theologically transformed universal viewpoint: i.e., to what can be intelligently understood and reasonably affirmed by a mind which is open to the possibilities of the transcendent, to the call of conversion, to the understanding and affirmation of the whole universe and all the possibilities of human development as the gift of a loving God.[2]

While that involves many other things as well, it does involve the historical-critical method of biblical interpretation.

To summarize, then: What we learn from St. Matthew about being transmitters of Christian tradition to our people is this: First, we should preach from the gospels;

second, we should apply them to the life-situation of our people; and third, we should use the best methods of interpretation we have, including modern biblical criticism. If we transmit the tradition in this way, our people will be able to sing with feeling the hymn that we have sung tonight:

Come, pure hearts, in sweetest measure
    Sing of those who spread the treasure
In the holy Gospels shrined;
    Blessed tidings of salvation,
Peace on earth their proclamation,
    Love from God to lost mankind.

See the rivers four that gladden,
    With their streams, the better Eden,
Planted by our Lord most dear;
    Christ the fountain, these the waters;
Drink, O Sion's sons and daughters,
    Drink and find salvation here.

The Hymnal (134)

2

Biblical Criticism
as Proclamation

Second Sunday after Christmas, 1972
Trinity, Wauwatosa
Gospel A

Many clergy are afraid to use the negative results of criticism in their sermons because they believe their people will find it too threatening. I think they may do so quite safely if they follow these three rules: (1) Do not bring them in gratuitously, but only to make a point. (2) They should not be used in a debunking, but in a constructive way. (3) It should be apparent to the congregation that the minister's own faith has not been diminished but rather strengthened by his use of biblical criticism. What follows is intended as a case in point.

I have made it a policy never to go to biblical movies or to read biblical novels. My reason is not that they are not good films or books or that they are not religiously edifying or anything like that; the reason is rather that I am a specialist and the author of the work usually is not, and so the whole thing usually sounds off key to me. You may remember a recent series of TV commercials in which a very chic and dignified woman was shown in the sort of pose in which she would sit for a formal portrait. After we had had a second or two to be impressed with her breeding and dignity she would say, "My girdle is killing me." That would spoil the whole effect. She was shown to be not some character from a plane high above that we all live on, but one who shared the annoying and everyday problems that plague most of the women in the audience. The effectiveness of the ad depended on the woman's stepping out of character and that can be a very effective gimmick if you plan it that way, but it is only embarrassing if you don't. The Bible scholar who reads biblical fiction is constantly confronted with characters who step out of character when the author didn't intend them to. As I say, the effect is rather like someone singing off key and not knowing it, and being a witness to that is an embarrassment I avoid as often as possible.

Thus I was only vaguely aware that a novel had been written in which Pontius Pilate was the main character and certainly the author's name was not familiar to me. Had it been then I would have been saved the bother. I was recently asked to review a new book called *The First Christmas: The True and Unfamiliar Story.* The caption goes on to say that this story is told "in words and pictures by Paul L. Maier." The only thing I knew about him was what it said on the back of the dustjacket under his picture, that he was a professor of history at Western Michigan and that his fields are ancient history and the Reformation. That sounded pretty good. I think the thing that really snared me into reading it was the pictures: There were a number of them, they were of places that I had recently visited, and they brought back a lot of memories. And there were also some photographs of astronomical phenomena and very scientific looking diagrams, obviously about the star of Bethlehem, and I don't know much about that sort of thing and so it all seemed like a pretty good bet.

It turned out to be a "Try it, you'll like it!" sort of

experience and I should have taken at least four Alka-Selt-zers. The book goes into fantastic historical detail about every aspect of the Christmas story. There are over two pages devoted to the question of whether the first Christmas could have been a white Christmas or not. Too bad the guy didn't wait a bit before publishing: Two inches of snow fell on Jerusalem on last Tuesday and that would have been good for an extra footnote. All this detail and the guy never gets around to questioning whether it all happened this way or not or whether there are any inconsistencies in the gospel accounts or not and, most important of all, he doesn't really try to find out what the gospel writers wanted to proclaim about Jesus—what the significance of any of the facts was. It was all rather as if someone had written a seven-volume study of the diet of a unicorn complete with tables from the Department of Agriculture without ever getting around to discussing whether there are such things as unicorns and why anybody would want to feed them if there were.

What Maier never takes seriously in his book is that only two of the four gospels have any information about the birth of Jesus and between those two accounts there are not only differences but even contradictions. Until that fact is recognized and faced up to, one cannot begin to understand these stories. Some of the differences are not inconsistent with one another. Luke tells of the Annunciation to Mary for instance and Matthew tells of the Annunciation to Joseph, but both could have happened. Only Matthew tells about wisemen, and only Luke tells about shepherds, but there is no inherent reason why both could not have come to worship the newborn Jesus. The real difficulty begins with Luke's dates. He gives us two indications of when Jesus was born. He tells us that Herod was the king but he also tells us that Joseph and Mary went to Bethlehem because of a decree of Augustus Caesar that a census should be taken for the purpose of constructing a tax roll. Luke tells us, "When the first census took place, Quirinius was governor of Syria." The trouble is that we know when Herod the Great lived and when Quirinius was governor of Syria and they are not the same time. Herod died in 4 BC and the census under Quirinius was taken in 6 AD, ten years later. We know that because the Jewish people were very superstitious about census-taking. When David had tried to take a census he almost had a revolt on his hands, and there *was* a revolt in 6 AD when Quirinius' census was taken. Since the Jews were so touchy about censuses, we can be sure that if any other census had been taken, or Quirinius had had an earlier term as governor we would know about it. One date has to be wrong. Since Matthew also mentions Herod, most scholars say that his time is the correct date and the one in connection with Quirinius' census is wrong.

But you see where that puts us. If Jesus was not born at the time of the census under Quirinius, the reason for Mary and Joseph to travel from Nazareth to Bethlehem disappears. And that brings us to a contradiction between Matthew and Luke. According to Matthew, Bethlehem was the home town of Joseph and Jesus was born there because Joseph and Mary were already living there, while according to Luke they were living in Nazareth and only went up to Bethlehem because of the census. Not only that, but Matthew tells of a flight into Egypt to avoid persecution, but Luke says that the Holy Family went straight home to Nazareth: "When they finished doing all that was required by the law of the Lord, they returned to Galilee, to their home town of Nazareth." (2:39).

So you see what is wrong with a book like the one I just read. It glosses over all the differences as though they did not exist. It fails to deal with the historical difficulties; it ignores their existence. It appears afraid of them, as if to admit that they exist would be to bring the whole Christian faith into question. But here we should remember what the Fourth Gospel has to tell us; in it Jesus says, "I am the Way, the Truth, and the Light." Now if Jesus is the truth, he has nothing to fear from truth, even the truth that the gospels tell contradictory stories about his birth. One way we could deal with this is to say that Matthew and Luke had incomplete information, that Matthew didn't know that Mary and Joseph lived in Nazareth before Jesus was born and that Luke didn't know that they had gone into Egypt after he was born.

I don't think this goes into the matter deeply enough though. We forget that people in the early Church were not stupid; they knew a contradiction when they saw one. If their concern had been to reconstruct the past the way that Truman Capote did in *In Cold Blood*, they would have eliminated all of the inconsistencies and contradictions, they would have smoothed over the rough edges and made it all fit. Their failure to do so indicates that they had some other purpose in mind in telling the story of the birth of Jesus the way they did.

Or rather, they had a number of other purposes. We can't explore them all, but we can look at a few that come up in today's gospel. If we do I think we'll find meaning far more profound than any speculation about whether the first Christmas could have been white.

One of the most obvious features of the gospel for today is the theme of the fulfillment of prophecy. We are told that the reason for the flight into Egypt was "to make come true what the Lord had said through the prophet. 'I called my Son out of Egypt.'" This is a quotation from Hosea 11:1. Then when Joseph made his home town in Nazareth we are told, "He did this to make come true what the prophet had said, 'He will be called a Nazarene.'" This verse does not appear in the Old Testament, but may be related to Isaiah 11:1. Our gospel today leaves out a section in the middle which tells of the slaughter of the Holy Innocents. The conclusion of that section is, "In this way what the prophet Jeremiah had said came true."

Now this is very important. One of the most striking characteristics of the whole gospel of Matthew is its use of these Old Testament proof texts as prophecies about Jesus. There are many in the other gospels and in the rest of the New Testament, but they are specially noticeable in Matthew. Not only that, Matthew arranges his gospel in such a way that it is divided into five parts, each with a narrative section and a teaching section. These five sections would have reminded any good Jew of the time of the first five books of the Old Testament that Moses was believed to have written. They were thought of as the most holy part of the Bible, the Torah or Law. In the first of the five sections in Matthew is the Sermon on the Mount and this mountain reminds us of Mt. Sinai where Moses received the Law. Jesus is obviously being set up by Matthew in parallel with Moses.

When we recognize that fact, all of the references to fulfilled prophecy in today's gospel begin to make sense. The Jews of Jesus' time were looking for a new redemption that would be as important for them as their delivery from the land of bondage in Egypt through the Exodus under Moses. And they also believed that there would be many parallels between this new redemption and the earlier one. Thus when Matthew tells of a flight into Egypt so that the prophecy can be fulfilled, "I called my Son out of Egypt," we are being told that Jesus is the new Moses, he is the one Israel has been expecting and longing for.

And this shows us why Matthew includes the story of the slaughter of the Holy Innocents. Jesus escaped a massacre of male Jewish infants in the same way that Moses was saved from a similar slaughter in Egypt by Pharaoh's daughter.

Matthew did not stop with saying that Jesus was as great as Moses; he goes on to make it clear that Moses was only a preview of coming attractions, a taste of what was to come. What was promised in Moses would be given in Jesus. This is the mighty proclamation of today's gospel. And it is good news indeed. And far more important to us than the question of whether the first Christmas was white.

3

Dealing with a Current Problem

The Last Sunday After the Ephiphany, 1973
Trinity, Wauwatosa
Gospel B

*Such terms as "life situation" and "situation in the
congregation" do not have an obvious content, and what
they mean can only be spelled out in practice. The
following sermon tried to take a subject that was on
everyone's mind and to use it to help people move beyond
their immediate preoccupations to deal with some more
serious considerations.*

All of the cartoonists suddenly seem to have had the
same idea at once. They show a man passing a meat
market in the window of which is a sign that says, "Ask
about our Eat Now Pay Later Plan." At the end of a
checkout counter in a grocery store is a loan officer from a
bank who will arrange long term payments for a week's
food supply. Beef is delivered at the supermarket in a
Brink's truck. But really, it's no laughing matter. The cost
of food rose 2.1% in January, the highest monthly increase
since the Korean war, and the President has admitted that
it will go up further in February. The administration
hopes that the increase for the entire year will be only six

percent; if it is that, then the price of food will have gone up by 43% in the last eleven years. There is no guarantee that the increase will be held down to six percent for the year though; it will be summer before the decline in prices is expected by the government and fall before beef goes down; by then new inflationary factors may have come into play. As this week's *Newsweek* says, "Even if Administration predictions are on the money, the results may not be evident until labor unions, incensed by the high cost of eating, smash through all reasonable wage guidelines in contract talks and tip the scales toward still more inflation."

Harried housewives are looking for ways of cutting costs. Meat is the big expense item—one Oconomowoc store this week was advertising rib roast at $1.38 per pound, t-bone at $1.84 and porterhouse at $1.89 (and this is supposed to be a sale!), although they were very low on ground beef: you could get it for only 79 cents a pound if you bought it in 5 pound bags. And there is no reason to expect meat to go down soon. It takes nineteen months to breed a steer and fatten it for market, so the supply is likely to stay down for a while. Then, too, the price of feeding cattle has increased tremendously; India and Russia have siphoned off our excess wheat and the price for it has gone up. The latest word is that Russia's winter wheat crop has failed this year and that American wheat in abundance will be called for there. Stock feeders are shifting to soybean meal, and the price of soybeans has increased by 126% in the past year. In spite of the cutthroat competition between supermarket chains, it looks like we can all get ready to say, "WEO, how A&P prices have changed!" in a sense not intended by the TV commercial.

So the poor wife looks for cheaper ways to serve her family protein. A gram of protein in dried lima beans costs only one-tenth of what it does in sirloin steak, but most wives are not prepared to go that far yet. The President recommended that people save money by eating cheese instead of meat, but right here in Wisconsin, the Dairy State, an investigation was conducted by the Milwaukee *Journal* which showed that processed cheese slices "are more expensive per unit of protein than hamburger." The only way you can save money using cheese is to make dishes that require less cheese than the amount of meat you would put in a meat dish. By doing that a woman may save as much as 32 cents per meal—if she doesn't blow it all on mixes for the casserole. One of the tips recently given on stretching your food dollar is: "Avoid certain convenience foods such as mixes designed to be sprinkled on poultry or added to meat—such as Hamburger Helper —before they are cooked. They are basically fillers, have relatively little food value, and are costly." Another traditional meat substitute has been fish but the Department of Agriculture has said that "fish prices are rising faster than almost anything else in the food basket" because of hurricane Agnes and, besides that, there is the fear of mercury poisoning that prompted the advice last summer that adults not eat fish caught out of Lake Michigan more than once a month. Even if you still like peanut butter, as I do, it's terribly fattening. And even milk and eggs have become dangerous through their cholesterol count. All I've got to say is that I'm glad I like chicken and have developed a tolerance for cottage cheese.

As disturbing as all this is to all of us, it has not yet become a religious issue in our discussion of it. That comes in our reaction to the situation. What are all of these wives going to do who go to the grocery store and find that they can no longer make ends meet on their food budget? We have a student at Nashotah House who was in the retail grocery business for a number of years before coming to seminary. When he decided that there had to be more to life than peddling groceries, he had a chain of about a dozen supermarkets. Once he discussed the loss from shoplifting in places like his with me and he said that in a low profit-margin business like the food business, the annual loss from shoplifting could wipe out all the profit. The most surprising information on the subject he gave me, though, concerned who did the stealing. He said that more often than not it was respectable housewives whose husbands had reasonably high-paying jobs. Given only a certain amount for household expenses, the only way they knew to stretch the budget was to steal from the grocery store.

Of course, only a few women will steal, but their doing so must be indicative of the anxiety many must feel at the best of times over their ability to cope with the demands made on their management of household finances. It seems to me inevitable that this normal anxiety is going to be increased severly by the present skyrocketing prices. That being so, the problem I want to focus on is the psychological feelings of guilt that so often accompany such anxiety. We all seem rather automatically to assume that if we are being good and God loves us, we will have no problems and everything will go smoothly for us. We will be able to pay all our bills and send the kids to college and even put money into the bank. That means that if anything goes wrong, God must be angry with us and the only thing that could make him angry is that we have done something that has displeased him. Not that we know what it was, because with God you are never sure. It's just that he has these rules that he has never told us and he is very unhappy if they are not obeyed, and he keeps close tabs on each of us to see if we are obeying them even if we don't know what they are. When he catches us stepping out of line, he zaps us. Well, all of us who mastered psychology through newsstand paperbacks know the explanation for all this: We have carried over neurotic patterns of guilt feelings from our childhood because they were programmed into us by authoritarian parents. After all, Freud told us that God is the national projection of the father image, and we expect God to treat us the way that our daddy did.

Since we can't engage in any depth therapy here (and I couldn't anywhere else either since I don't have the training), let's deal with this question in a brief but theological way. The gospel for today is the story of the transfiguration. If we have Jesus' success story anywhere in the gospels, this is it. Just as mild-mannered reporter Clark Kent can duck into a phone booth and reveal that appearances are deceiving, that he really is Superman, Jesus revealed on the mountain that he is God. This is the only time before the resurrection that his incognito was broken. It is so out of tune with the rest of the story of his life that many New Testament scholars think that the transfiguration is really the story of a resurrection appearance of Jesus that got put into the middle of the gospel by mistake instead of at the end where it belongs. There are a number of technical reasons why I disagree with them, but we don't need to go into them here. Instead, we need only to make the point that this story is not so exclusively one of success as we had imagined. The place in the gospel it is told is just after Jesus has announced that he is going to have to go to Jerusalem to be put to death at the instigation of the religious leaders of Israel. When on the mountain of transfiguration Peter is swept away by the glory of the occasion and wants to build shrines and stay there forever, Jesus tells him that they have to go down into the valley again, that he still has to go on to Jerusalem to die. Indeed, St. Luke tells us that when Moses and Elijah appeared to Jesus on the mountain, it was his death that they discussed with him.

The point is this: If all the suffering was not taken out of the life of the only perfect man who ever lived; if, in fact, it was in his very suffering that his perfection was most manifest, then we cannot simply equate difficulty in this life with divine disfavor nor can we identify ease in this life as a sign of divine approval. We Americans have the highest standard of living on earth. Even now, the financial hardships we are threatened by would seem like undreamed-of luxury to most of the rest of the people on earth. Our affluence does not prove that we are God's favorite nation and the loss of it would be no indication that he was punishing us. During this time of anxiety, though, we might be comforted by a prayer for trustfulness taken from the order for Family Prayer in the Prayer Book:

O most loving Father, who willest us to give thanks for all things, to dread nothing but the loss of thee, and to cast all our care on thee who carest for us; Preserve us from faithless fears and worldly anxieties and grant that no clouds of this mortal life may hide from us the light of that love which is immortal, and which thou has manifested unto us in thy Son, Jesus Christ our Lord. Amen.

4

Preaching on a Political Issue

The Fourth Sunday of Easter, 1973
Trinity, Wauwatosa
Gospel B

A very real situation in the life of the congregation may arise in the political area and the minister may feel at a loss about how to deal with it. On the one hand, he wishes to avoid being partisan, appearing to give the Church's stamp of approval to human movements that are always transient and in danger of falling into sin, and afraid, too, of offending parishioners who may have honest convictions that disagree with those of the minister, and, on the other hand, he knows that not to speak out is to be derelict in responsibility and cowardly. The sermon below was an effort to reflect on the Watergate scandal shortly after it broke without passing premature judgment on any of its characters.

In the past few weeks the nation has been shocked to see what was once described as a "third-rate burglary" grow into such a scandal that 30 percent of the people of the country have been polled as believing that if the President either knew about the burglary beforehand or had a part in covering it up, he should be impeached. We have heard the stories unfold one after another. John Dean said that the President congratulated him back in September for his help in covering up White House involvement in wiretapping. Men on the White House payroll broke into the office of a psychiatrist to get evidence against Daniel Ellsberg, who released the Pentagon papers to the press. Because of this government misconduct, charges against Ellsberg have been dismissed and he is intending to sue the President for conspiracy to deprive him of his civil liberties. A Presidential staff member offered the judge at the Ellsberg trial the job of being director of the FBI, apparently as a bribe, doing so at a meeting at which the President put in a brief appearance. At the order of the Attorney General the phones of reporters and White House aides have been tapped over the last four years in an effort to stop leaks of government information to the press. Funds for the Campaign to Re-elect the President have been used to pay the Watergate defendants to remain silent. Funds from the same source were used to pay for a number of "dirty tricks" against Democratic candidates. The ex-Attorney General has been indicted on charges of fraud for interceding with the Securities and Exchange Commission for a man who had stolen $224 million from a mutual fund and made a donation of about $\frac{1}{10}$ of one percent of that amount to the President's re-election campaign. The majority of ranking members of the President's staff have resigned.

Now, I don't know any more than you do about whether the President had any knowledge of any involvement in any of this and Christian charity as well as democratic practice requires that we treat him as innocent unless he is proved guilty, so we aren't going to talk about him this morning; we are only going to talk about his staff members who have been shown to be guilty. And we are not even going to beat that dead horse very much, because no moral progress is made by our feeling superior to the lapses of others. The only reason for us to study the sin of anyone else is to see if our doing so won't help us to recognize some sin of our own; we can't change the morals of public figures, but we can change our own.

The question we need to begin with is one phrased in this week's *Time* magazine: "How could such pervasive corruption of ethics start in an Administration of such seemingly square-shooting disciples of law and order?" I think the answer to that question comes out in the President's defense of these men: They were, he said, "men whose zeal exceeded their judgment, and who may have done wrong in a cause they deeply believed to be right." This cause was the campaign for the re-election of the President. The President went on to say: "It can be very easy under the intensive pressures of a campaign for even well-intentioned people to fall into shady practices . . . and both of our great parties have been guilty of such practices." The response of *Time* magazine to this statement was:

While there is obviously plenty of political corruption on all sides, there is no evidence that Democrats—or other Republicans—burglarized offices, tapped telephones, kept huge caches of secret campaign funds to finance the disruption of opponents' campaigns, or tried to obstruct the judicial system's attempts to punish the offenders.

This is to say that in the past political corruption has usually been the efforts of venal men to line their own pockets. They were crooks and they knew it. What is different about Watergate is that it was the well-intentioned who fell into shady practices; they did wrong in a cause they deeply believed to be right. To put it another and more familiar way: They were men who forgot that the end does not justify the means.

But, as I said, it is our own sins that we need to

remember this morning, not those of people who will never have access to our superior moral insights. There is a kind of evil that only the high-minded are capable of. They think they have the best interests of the people at heart and that justifies their doing what has to be done in order to put their program across. Church history is full of religious leaders who have fallen into this trap. Many do so in politics at the local level. "We of the better element in the community need to take steps to protect our city from the riff-raff." Husband and wife have manipulated one another and parents have exploited their children in this same confidence of righteousness.

The gospel for today deals with this kind of problem. It is the parable of the Good Shepherd. In the part that was read at the Eucharist a contrast is made between the Good Shepherd, who owns the sheep and has deep interest in them, and the hired hand, who runs away when he sees the wolf coming because the only reason he looks after the sheep is that he is paid to do so. Now in our political analogy the hired hand could be compared to the classical corrupt politician, whose only interest in his constituents is in what he can get out of them. But the whole parable was not read this morning, and the hired hands are not the only villains in it. The three verses before the ones we heard in church go like this:

All others who came before me are thieves and robbers; but the sheep do not listen to them . . . The thief comes only in order to steal, kill, and destroy. I have come in order that (the sheep) might have life, life in all its fullness.

Throughout the gospel it is clear who the thieves and robbers are; they are the members of the religious establishment. They think that they have God in a box and that no one else has any knowledge of what God is like; anyone who wants God must get him from them. Thus they are unable to recognize Jesus as the one who comes from God. Rather, they consider him the enemy of true religion, and to serve God they have Jesus put to death. Thus we come to see again that the worst sin of all is pride. It is far more dangerous than the sins of the flesh: avarice, gluttony, wrath, and lust. Those who commit them usually know that they are sinning, but the man who is guilty of pride can be self-righteous about the most heinous of crimes; when he does it it is no longer a crime because he is one of the good guys and therefore anything he does must be good. When we lose all capacity for self-criticism we are irreformable; there is no saving us. I hope, then, that Watergate can point out to all of us the danger of considering our purposes to be so lofty that they justify extraordinary measures for their accomplishment.

5

The Spirit of the Times

The Twenty-first Sunday after Pentecost, 1972
Trinity, Wauwatosa
Gospel A

Sometimes the most obvious situation of the congregation is the mood of the entire nation and that mood may call for theological reflection and even moral exhortation. The media can help the preacher discern this sort of sign of the times.

The news magazines that I read all seemed this week to be trying to zero in on something about the state of the national consciousness right now. The cover article in *Newsweek* was billed as "Yearning for the 50's: the Good Old Days." The article appeared in the Life and Leisure section and dealt more than anything else with the current revival of rock and roll music, although there was also an inset on the great interest these days in Marilyn Monroe. Why the 50's should be regarded as a golden age is an interesting question. Jeff Greenfield, who has written a book called *Where Have You Gone, Joe DiMaggio?*, says that one reason is that another generation has grown older and is merely looking back on its youth with nostalgia. Not that everything from the period is to be recalled. As

Newsweek comments: "To a lot of people, the '50's evoke such grim memories as Korea, Suez, Hungary, Sputnik, and economic recession. It was a time of economic recession and sexual repression, of cold war and Communist hunting, and for blacks it was a time of almost total exclusion from the white consciousness." Even Greenfield says that not everything in the 50's is worth reviving: "There's no Joe McCarthy revival, and nobody is longing for the days of the H-bomb tests." But what does seem to be longed for is the ability to live with such problems and ignore them. As Walter Iooss, Jr., has said, "There were plenty of problems in the world but nobody cared. All we worried about were cars, records, and who broke up with whom."

This week's "Time Essay" suggests that we are doing a pretty good job of being able to close our eyes to the problems going on around us. In its title the essay asks, "Is Nobody Indignant Anymore?" It deals with the lack of public outrage at recent political scandals and sees perhaps some maturity involved in the disappearance of unreal expectations of our politicians, but says that something very valuable may be in danger of being lost here. Listen to the concluding words of the essay:

Perhaps in some strange way the absence of outrage signals a slightly weary realism about how politics and other enterprises really function—a psychological intersection of public and private moralities, a sense that the men in Washington and their friends are only doing what everyone else does, only bigger and better. A little cheating, after all, is a drearily popular habit—from parking tickets to overtime cards to expense accounts. . . . But there is a somewhat depressing loss of innocence in failing to expect more from the nation's public officials. Somewhere in all of this huge indifference, the principle of moral leadership may be sinking without a trace.

In a column in *Newsweek* called "The Big Sleep," Shana

Alexander tells about the shock she recently had driving on the freeways of Southern California: "How odd that all the bumper stickers have disappeared. Four years ago the freeway was a dense verbal thicket, a wild cacophony, often irreverent, of politics and patriotism and partisan humor. Today you can drive 100 miles and not see a single glue-on opinion of any kind. Have people grown up, shut up, or quit having opinions?" Her answer to that question is that people have quit having opinions.

Every time America goes on a binge, she must go away and sleep it off. After the exertion of World War I came the fun era of the roaring '20's, when Harding and Coolidge put everyone to sleep. In the '50's we rested up after World War II and the frantic '40's. The '60's were another binge—riots, assassinations, rotting cities, screaming sirens, and ever-widening war. So, sh-h-h-h. The country is sleeping now.

The Church has had its own problems of people wishing to sleep instead of dealing with the pressing moral demands that are made on them. A case in point comes up in our gospel for today. The story as it was read is one of the strangest in the New Testament. It is a parable told by Jesus about a king whose son was getting married. Being a king he had a lot of social obligations and so he sent out a lot of invitations. In those days when people were invited to a banquet, their host would send one of his slaves to escort each guest from his home to the place where the dinner was being held. When the king did this, none of the guests was ready; they wanted to put off coming. The king sent the slaves back and then the people who were invited got very rude indeed; some went off on various errands and some of them even went so far as to kill his slaves. This made the king so angry that he sent his army off to destroy the murderers and burn up their homes. Then he said, "I'm going to teach the others a lesson. They were planning on coming late to my party, but I'm going to see that there is no room left at the social event of the season when they arrive stylishly late. Go out and round up all the bums from the park benches. Go down on Skid Row and pick up all the drunks. Clean out the cells in the jails and bring all the prisoners over here. I am going to see that all of the seats at the table are filled and there won't be any room for any late-comers."

Now all of that makes enough sense for us to be able to follow it well enough, but now comes the strange part. When all the derelicts had been herded into the banquet hall and it got to be time for the king to go down and fraternize with his guests he noticed that one of them didn't have on a wedding garment. Now this doesn't mean that he hadn't taken the time and trouble to go to Sherkow's and rent an After Six midnight blue tuxedo complete with cummerbund and ruffled shirt. It means only that he did not have on a newly laundered garment, but still, that's a lot to expect. Where are you going to get a clean shirt on a park bench; you're lucky to have a shirt at all. So what does the king do? He tells his slave, "Throw this bum out of here!" The king should have known what the sartorial standards of transients are, and if he hadn't wanted anyone dressed like that at his feast, he should never have invited one. It sounds completely irrational.

Until we come upon the explanation of what has happened here. Originally this was not one but two parables, one about the host who invited the wayfarers to take the places at his table that those on the original guest list had been dilatory about filling. The other parable is limited to having someone throw a real white tie affair at which someone shows up in a bowling shirt and tennis shoes. The reason that the two parables were stuck together was that Matthew got worried about the meaning of the first parable. It sounded as though there were no requirements to be met by those who entered the kingdom of God. The messianic banquet was being treated as a

"Come as you are" party. He knew the other parable, which suggests that if we cooperate with God, we must do so on his terms, and he added it to the first one. As the great scholar of the parables, Joachim Jeremias, has said: "In the course of its missionary activity, the Church was continually confronted by the danger that the gospel of the free grace of God might be interpreted as freeing the baptized from their moral responsibilities. . . . In order to remove any ground for such a misunderstanding, the parable of the Wedding Garment was inserted into the parable of the Great Supper, introducing the principle of merit, and emphasizing the necessity for repentance as the condition of acquittal at the Last Judgment." [1] This same warning is very appropriate to our country now in a time when it is trying to back away from moral responsibility and become uninvolved in anything that might make demands on it.

Using Media Events

The media have their ears very close to the ground so that one may assume that when a book, a play, a record, a film, or what have you is a big hit, it is dealing with something that is in the forefront of the consciousness of the people and is, therefore, something that is worthy of theological analysis. It would be tiresome if we preached about nothing but best-sellers and hits, but occasionally one offers a natural entrée into what a sermon should be dealing with. It is hard to say, though, whether popular "religious" successes offer more pitfalls or handholds.

On a Saturday night in mid-November, Father Jacobus was reading his evening paper and came across an article by the *Journal*'s music and theatre critic, Dominique Paul Noth, about a new rock opera called *Jesus Christ—Superstar*. As a priest and as a young man attuned to the music of today, Father Jacobus was quite excited by the article. Noth admitted that he was a critic of rock rather than church music and limited his evaluation to the music, which he found to be good. But he went on to say that

Jesus Christ—Superstar deserves and needs to be heard, "both in and out of a church setting." He predicted that it would make enemies among the traditionalists, but suggested that it could make converts, "especially among the young." That was all Father Jacobus needed to hear. He immediately began phoning all the record stores he knew and none of them had it in stock. Most of them had not even heard of it and thought the call was some kind of prank. Finally, though, he found it at Sears and rushed out to get a copy.

That was way back in November and you know what has happened since. For the past several weeks the album, which had been among the best-sellers for some time, has occupied first place on the local hit parade. Reactions have been mixed, as one would expect. The conservative magazine, *Christianity Today*, carries in its current issue both an article on the general popularity of what is called "Jesus Rock"—which has had its own rock festivals with thousands of spectators—and an editorial on the appropriateness of such music for religious use. It concludes:

To some, the medium of rock (hard, soft, or folk) depreciates the message. But to most young people of today it apparently enhances the message. That being the case, the witnessing potential of new sounds in music is no myth. As hungry young people search for the true bread, these new sounds can provide good soul food if tied in with the authentic Gospel.[1]

The *National Catholic Reporter* took account of the mixed reaction by having two reviews, one positive and the other negative. The negative one saw it as a pseudo-event created by mass media for a fast buck. It speaks of a nightmare of the reviewer in which the latest fad would be Christianity, on the basis, apparently, that it's so out that it is in. The new fad would be launched by John Lennon and Yoko Ono appearing at Westminster Abbey in sackcloth and ashes to announce their conversion to a regiment of reporters. There would then be spontaneous mass gatherings and reports on the CBS evening news, and cover stories in *Time, Newsweek,* and *Life.* In such a situation the production of a passion play in an imitation of contemporary music could really rake in the dough. The other reviewer compares *Jesus Christ—Superstar* very favorably to the work of Johann Sebastian Bach and Jonathan Swift.

Since you have undoubtedly been reading about it and—if you have teenage children—have probably heard some of it at least as background noise, it's not inappropriate for us to think about it this morning. It would be pointless for us to evaluate the music. Obviously it appeals to a lot of people. But we can deal with the question I get asked a lot in my capacity as a New Testament scholar: How close is the story to what the gospels have to say about Jesus' last days on earth?

For an example we can look at the Last Supper. At first it sounds as though the emphasis is startlingly different from the gospels. Instead of the institution of a sacrament what we have here appears more like a crying jag. The apostles have discovered that "malt can do more than Milton can to justify God's ways to man."

Look at all my trials and tribulations
Sinking in a gentle pool of wine
Don't disturb me now I can see the answers
Till this evening is this morning life is fine.

In the wine's warm glow, they have the confidence to look at their careers and believe that their ambitions will not be frustrated.

Always hoped that I'd be an apostle
Knew that I would make it if I tried
Then when we retire we can write the gospels
So they'll still talk about us when we've died

Jesus' response is also not what you'd expect:

The end . . .
Is just a little harder when brought about by friends
For all you care this wine could be my blood
For all you care this bread could be my body

The self-absorption of the apostles leaves them no attention to devote to the approaching catastrophe of their
master.

The end!
This is my blood you drink
This is my body you eat
If you would remember me when you eat and drink . . .
I must be mad thinking I'll be remembered—yes
I must be out of my head!
Look at your blank faces! My name will mean nothing
Ten minutes after I'm dead!
One of you denies me
One of you betrays me—

At first it sounds as though Jesus were only an ordinary
celebrity, depressed at his last hour by the fickleness of
fame. But then we see that the real question for him is
how such egoists as the apostles can possibly carry on his
work after his death. The institution of a sacrament is not
here, but what is here certainly has its place in the gospels.

It has its place, for instance, in our gospel for today. The
story is one of Jesus' three passion predictions in Mark. All
three of them follow a pattern. Jesus tells his disciples that
he is going to die. They respond in a completely inappropriate way—one that shows that they are much more
interested in their own ambitions than in his suffering.
Then someone who is not a disciple makes an appropriate
response to Jesus and Jesus follows this all up by some
teaching on the subject of his death. In our gospel for
today we get just the first two of these elements. Jesus
announces his approaching death. As soon as he finishes
speaking James and John come up to him and ask that

when he sits on his throne in his glorious kingdom they may be his top two assistants—his Kissinger and his Rogers.

This has to be one of the supreme examples of bad taste in history, one to rank with the reporter in the sick joke who asked "Other than that, Mrs. Lincoln, how did you enjoy the play?" or the little boy who personified *chutzpah* by killing his parents and then begging the mercy of the court because he was an orphan.

It is precisely this willingness of the apostles to plan their careers when Jesus' very life is at stake that *Jesus Christ—Superstar* displays so clearly in the Last Supper scene. With great dramatic skill the rock opera suddenly presents us with a psychologically plausible picture of the shocking self-absorption of the apostles. The gospels tell us of it, but somehow we seem to miss it. We know that the apostles were saints and saints aren't selfish. But the rock opera removes the sugar coating that piety has placed over the gospels and shows us that disciples can betray the Lord and they can deny him. And in showing us that it shows us also that we too can and do deny and betray him.

It took Jesus' death to change the selfish apostles. After that they could learn the truth of what he said to them after James and John asked him to grant their requests:

You know that the men who are considered rulers of the people have power over them and the leaders rule over them. This, however, is not the way it is among you. If one of you wants to be great, he must be the servant of the rest; and if one of you wants to be first, he must be the slave of all. For even the Son of Man did not come to be served; he came to serve and to give his life to redeem many people.

The disciples learned this and did indeed come to drink the cup that Jesus drank and to be baptized with the baptism with which Jesus was baptized. But how much of the Church since their time has lived in this knowledge?

The dean of American New Testament scholars, Frederick C. Grant, has come to this sad conclusion:

This is the tragedy, that a gospel meant for the healing of the nations accepted a lesser role and became only one more of 'the world's great religions,' leaving Hatred, War, Greed, Hunger, and Misery still the permanent rulers of mankind; and instead of one united body of believers it became a fissiparous crowd of competing sects, which preferred to do nothing rather than cooperate for the good of the human race or even for their own advantage. That is the tragedy, over which God himself must weep.[2]

The good thing about *Jesus Christ—Superstar* is that it can occasionally remind us of this tragedy and of our own role in it. And when we know, maybe we'll change.

7

"A Luminous Piece of Reality"

The First Sunday in Lent, 1971
Trinity, Wauwatosa
Gospel C

The phrase of the title comes from Clement Welsh of the College of Preachers. He uses it to refer to the slice of life that a playwright holds out for exploration as a way of making a serious comment on life as a whole. The selection is judicious to the extent that it permits a sure and direct move to the wider consideration. The preacher can also find such slices of life, and they make good points of departure for sermons. I thought that the news story about morals and manners in Las Vegas was luminous in this way.

Life is so confusing now that it's very seldom that we can look at any event and say, "This is good," or "That's bad." Every once in a while, though, something happens that is not only understandable in itself but is also a window into a lot else that is going on. Such an event, I believe, has occurred recently in Nevada. Las Vegas is probably the best publicized sin city in the country. The general idea seems to be that whatever you want, you can get it there. And now word comes out that prostitution has been banned there. So that means there has been a great triumph of morality and decency, right? Well, not quite. You see, the district attorney was trying to draw up an ordinance that would legalize prostitution. He already had a majority of the county commissioners on his side and it looked like a sure thing. But what stopped him was no sudden crusade launched by the better element in the community. Rather, the city's Convention Authority leaped into the breach. "One thing that we are fighting in booking conventions," they said, "is the image of Las Vegas. If we legalize it, it would really hurt us." And so it was not morals but business that caused the Nevada legislature to pass a law banning houses of prostitution— not in the whole state, but only in counties with a population over 200,000. The only county in the state with such a population is that in which Las Vegas is located.

The general idea seems to be that Las Vegas is wide open to attract tourists. But it can't be too wide open or tourists won't come. What I want us to look at here is not the morality of Las Vegas but that of the tourists. It sounds like they want to make sin a spectator sport. They want to do things that are racy enough to make them feel daring, but not enough to get them involved. What it reminds me of more than anything else is the distinction that Daniel Boorstin makes between "travellers" and "tourists" in his brilliant book, *The Image: A Guide to Pseudo-Events in America.* Travellers, according to Boorstin, go off on their own to see strange places and expose themselves to a certain amount of risk in their desire to acquire a first-hand knowledge of foreign people and things. The tourist, on the other hand, has someone else arrange his trip so that he can go to new places with the safety of staying at home; he stays in American hotels, has English-speaking guides, and no real contact with the natives. He appears in someone else's country as an observer rather than as a participant in the life there. It is as though he were transported through the world in an airtight transparent plastic container so that he was at all times shielded from the very life that he had travelled to see. The Convention Authority of Las Vegas seems to be offering guided tours to Sodom and Gomorrah on which one can enjoy the titillation of seeing all that sin without ever being exposed to the risk of becoming involved in it.

This concept of sin as a sport at which we would all like to be spectators is one of the reasons why we are so poorly prepared for understanding our gospel for today. We for whom sin has become a pseudo-event to be enjoyed only vicariously find it hard to see why the temptation of Jesus is such a big thing in the gospels. Yet in the theology of the gospels the temptation of Jesus ranks second only to the crucifixion and resurrection in its saving significance. The gospels are dominated by a worldview which thinks of time as divided into two parts, "the present age" and the "age to come." The present age is roughly BC and the age to come is AD. In the present age the universe was thought of as being under the control of the forces of evil, the demonic powers. Their rule would be brought to an end by the ushering in of the rule or reign or kingdom of God. But the shift of the ages would not be accomplished without a struggle; a pitched battle between the forces of good and those of evil would have to occur before the evil age would be at an end and the kingdom of God would be present in power. This war was expected to involve people to a certain degree but was also expected to be fought out between angels and devils and God and Satan. In the gospels the temptation of Jesus is regarded as the opening skirmish in that war of good and evil. The crucifixion was the decisive battle.

But in our world of sanitarily packaged sin at Las Vegas we find it hard to imagine the world in the grips of a real evil that is a terrifying threat. And we have the same trouble with Lent that we have with the temptation of

Jesus. Why spend forty days or even forty seconds in penitence for our sins when we have been too timid to have any? Which of us has been aware of being engaged in hand-to-hand combat with demons? How many of us know what it is to be afraid of sin, to feel that not hell but sin itself is a burning pit and that we are teetering on the edge?

To talk this way is to sound like Alice in the TV ad, who always has to make a big production out of everything. Our own experience has been so antiseptic that we have grown rather like Celia in *The Cocktail Party*:

Well, my bringing up was pretty conventional—
I had always been taught to disbelieve in sin.
Oh, I don't mean that it was ever mentioned!
But anything wrong from our point of view,
Was either bad form, or was psychological.
And bad form always led to disaster
Because the people one knew disapproved of it.

Most of us have long since ceased to be puritans. The sins the revivalist preached against seem to us no sins at all. Everyone we know drinks and dances and plays cards, breaks the Sabbath and takes the Lord's name in vain. And, of course, we have not been hoodwinked by the radicals into thinking that we have any corporate guilt for the racism, poverty, and war they say are going on but which somehow do not seem to impinge upon our lives.

About the only thing we are left with in Lent is the opportunity to lacerate our psychological guilt, scratching away at vague but persistent emotional itches. The classical Freudian explanation for these guilt feelings is that as children we were little animals with our full set of appetites, but that society in the form of our parents began to impose its rules upon us. The conflict between our wishes and their rules was resolved in our unconscious minds by a pretense of accepting our parents' rules as our own. But this left an internal conflict between what we wanted to do as animals and what we wanted to do as members of society. Since we never did as nobly as members of society as we had told ourselves we ought to, the only pleasure we had left was punishing ourselves for having done no better. Lent has been a good way to do that.

So we are left, not believing in sin, but considering everything wrong as being either bad form or psychological kinks. The gospel, which tells us that even the Son of God could be tempted, means nothing to us. I wonder if a good way for us to spend Lent may not be to go back over the sins that we have ceased to believe in—both the sins of the flesh and the social sins—and see if we are not more involved than we thought we were. If we do this we might be less likely to give Las Vegas a clean bill of health because prostitution is illegal there. We might even come to see how powerful the forces of evil are in our own lives and realize that it took the power of God himself to dethrone them from their control of the world.

8

Sharing Yourself

The First Sunday after the Epiphany, 1973
Trinity, Wauwatosa
Gospel B

Many people have guilt feelings about any doubts or questions they have concerning what they consider to be the traditional beliefs of their religion, and they try to pretend that these doubts do not exist. One way to help get such matters out into the open and dealt with before they undermine the whole basis of faith is for the minister to speak honestly about his own efforts to maintain his faith in the modern world, and about how these efforts affect some of the older ways of phrasing the content of belief. Many will then be greatly relieved because they will decide that if it is all right for the clergyman to have doubts, it is all right for them, too. This, of course, can be taken too far and the result will only be that the congregation will decide that the minister is sailing under false colors as an official spokesman of a belief that he does not hold.

This morning I want to try something a little bit different. The format will not be altered all that much; the change is going to be in the kind of content we have. In the past I have usually tried to give you something that I had thought through and come to some kind of conclusion on, but this morning we are going to try something unfinished. I haven't got this into final shape for my own satisfaction yet, so this morning you are invited to share in the process rather than the results. Maybe we can do a little theological jamming together and see what we come up with.

We'll start with the problem. It may be entirely personal with me and may not be felt by any of the rest of you. If that's the case, then maybe you can help me. Or maybe it should be a problem for you and I can help make it one. We'll see. My problem is that much theological language no longer means anything very specific to me; maybe it never did and I am just now realizing it or maybe it did and now does so no longer. Please don't misunderstand me about this. I am not trying to say that I've lost my faith; if anything, that's stronger than ever. I don't have any complaints about religious experience. My dissatisfaction is entirely with theological language.

Let me give you an example. If a Jesus freak were to stop me on the street and say to me, "Jesus saves!" my most likely response would be to say, "Moses invests!" What I would mean by that was that I rejected his entire language. While it is true that my basic understanding of myself and the world comes to me through my experience of being a member of the Christian Church, telling me that Jesus has saved me does not allude to any reality I know. To say "Jesus saves" is to say that by undergoing a dramatic conversion experience I can escape hell and go to heaven. That may be perfectly true but that's not where I live. In a way, it's like telling me that if I wear a copper bracelet a meteorite won't fall on my head or if I snap fingers like this, it will keep the elephants away.

Having stated the problem, I now want to begin to try to sketch in a provisional solution, and that may be the only kind of solution we ever get for something like this. This particular solution began for me when I read an article that was supposed to be satirical in the November issue of *Psychology Today*; the article had the thesis that most politicians, and presidents especially—whatever party they come from—do not solve problems in a practical way, but approach them the way that medicine men or shamans of primitive tribes do. The writer tells us, "When they are faced with societal ills, the President, the Congress, the governors, and the mayors gesticulate grandly, and emit fantastic noises—usually a series of promises and threats—but nothing much ever comes of all this. Their chiefs are like rainmakers during a rather dry season." [1]

While all of this seems likely enough to me, it was another part of the article that caught my attention. This refers to one of the shamanistic techniques that politicians employ. We read: "With . . . problems that are imaginary to begin with, the changing of a name (a typical magical procedure employed to ward off the evil eye), often helps. This magic is most frequently practiced in foreign policy." [2] The example given was our relations toward Red China. Since the end of World War II, we have assumed that we could not have anything to do with that country. Now we are opening relations. As the article says,

The events of 1963 and 1972 did not reflect sudden changes in the economic-sociopolitical structure of the USSR or Red China. Rather, two Presidents and their aides, for reasons of their own, decided it was time to deemphasize the old demons. They then engaged in exchanges of gifts, ceremonial meals, public hugs, mutual visits, and new nomenclature for the Communist bloc, and they succeeded in allaying many of the fears of Americans (and probably those of many Russians and Chinese). [3]

Now what I want to say about this technique of

changing the reality of something by changing the name we call it by is not at all satirical but is intended very seriously. What I want to say about it is that it works. Look at it in terms of the very example proposed. There is no reality of China that is independent of what we call her. It is not that China was harmless all along and we just now got around to recognizing the fact. Rather, it was the attitudes of the two nations toward one another that was the reality; as long as they mistrusted one another, each was dangerous. Now that they do trust one another—if they do—they are not dangerous. We don't have an unchanging reality and a changing name. The name is the reality and when the name is changed the reality is changed.

O.K., now let's apply that to religious language. The gospel for today, as you remember, is the story of the baptism of Jesus. The reason that we had that story on this particular day is that it is regarded as an epiphany, a manifestation of Jesus' divine nature. This manifestation came when the voice from heaven said, "You are my own dear Son. I am well pleased with you." But that is not the part of the story we're interested in right now. The part I want to deal with is the question of why Jesus was baptized in the first place. John's baptism was for the remission of sins and yet Jesus was supposed to be sinless; why did he need to be baptized? Matthew felt this as strongly as we do, so when he retold this story, he changed it and had John the Baptist tell Jesus that he should be baptized by him, but Jesus' answer that his being baptized would fulfill all righteousness still doesn't really tell us why the one who was without sin should receive the baptism for the remission of sins.

I think we can understand it, though, if we recognize that by being baptized Jesus was changing his name from that of sinless to sinner. The one who had no sin was to accept the fate of sinners. And by identifying himself with sinners, he made it possible for us to identify with his sinlessness. This makes it possible for God to change our names. Through Jesus, God no longer has to call us sinners; he can call us righteous. This is not all there is to it, but it is an important part. It is by this shamanistic technique of name-changing that we are made righteous.

Now nothing we have said so far is too surprising. Martin Luther, among other people, has said all this already. But what they have not said—or at least not so that I could understand it—is that by changing the name we really do change the reality.

Let me show how that works in something that is a little less all-encompassing than the contrast between sin and righteousness. Let's look at something that is big enough in its way, but still much simpler and easier to identify. Let's take alcoholism. We are told that the one necessary step in recovering from alcoholism is for the person who has it to admit to himself that he does. As long as he can continue to kid himself and say, "I can quit anytime I want to," he will go from bad to worse. It is when he admits that he is sick, that he has a disease, and that he is not able to drink in moderation like other people that he can begin to control his drinking. By changing the name that he applies to himself, he changes the reality. He does not cease to be an alcoholic, but he does become an alcoholic who remains sober.

And when God changes the name by which he calls us from sinner to righteous, it does not mean that we suddenly become different creatures. We do not become saints; we become sinners who are on the wagon as far as sin is concerned. Walker Percy has a beautiful example in his novel, *Love in the Ruins.* The sub-title is "A Bad Catholic Near the End of the World." The bad Catholic has stopped going to church and is continually getting drunk and committing adultery. At the end of the book, though, he is back in a state of grace but that does not mean that he ceases to be tempted or even to sin. Celebrating his restoration to the Church on Christmas he is saved from adultery only by an interruption and he falls off the wagon for the first time in six months, but by changing his name from being out of grace to being in grace he has changed the whole dynamic of his life. Now this is a kind of religious language that I don't have any trouble with.

9

Attitude Alteration

The Eighteenth Sunday after Trinity, 1972
Trinity, Wauwatosa
Gospel A

When dealing with fundamental attitudes that people have, it is often not a wise policy to attack those beliefs directly. A much wiser approach is to deal with other things that can be considered in a more or less value-free way, but which nevertheless have implications for the attitudes under consideration.

Most of us did not have to read Alvin Toffler's *Future Shock* in order to discover that change is taking place in our society at a rate that is faster than our human capacity to adapt. We knew enough about that already, thank you. Our difficulty was not in arriving at the insight, but in avoiding becoming merely another statistic to document the thesis that people can't cope with so much change. What we need is something to help us deal with the change, some island of security and immutability on which we can firmly plant our feet in the middle of the sea of change. And many of us had hoped that the Church would be that island for us. Those of us who did have been disappointed, because the Church has appeared as unstable and as kaleidoscopically variable as everything else in our society. On a national scale we have heard of theological changes that have moved from the death to the resurrection of God. During the sixties many seemed to think that the essence of the church lay in its contribution to social reform. And all of Christendom has gone through the unsettling experience of new forms of worship. Roman Catholics had to become accustomed to doing without Latin, "mainline" Protestant churches have had members who spoke in tongues, and Episcopalians have had to come to terms with the Green Book. Even in a parish that has been as liturgically conservative as Trinity, we have had the altar moved out from the wall, the priest now has his face rather than his back to the congregation, and the elements for Holy Communion are brought up from the rear by adults rather than over from the credence by an acolyte. Change is as characteristic of life in Church as it is of every other aspect of our lives in the final minutes of the third quarter of the twentieth century.

Recently, though, there has come some evidence that all change is not for the worse—that there even may be such a thing as progress—and it has come from an unexpected quarter. A couple of weeks ago there was a vast conference of theological scholars, some 3,000 of them from all over the world, that met in Los Angeles. One of the selected speakers who addressed the entire gathering was a Roman Catholic Old Testament scholar from DePaul University in Chicago. His name is John McKenzie, and he is one of the most respected biblical authorities in the Catholic Church. Yet what Father McKenzie talked about was changing concepts of God in the Old Testament period. There is no doubt that the Jewish idea of what God is like changed a great deal during the time that the Old Testament was being written. These ancient ideas are still there in the Old Testament to be read, although, as

Father McKenzie said, "Some traces of the early Yahweh remain which the heir of the Judaeo-Christian tradition would prefer not to have brought out of the closet; it is something like publishing the fact that grandfather was a horsethief." [1]

Of course, the worst Jewish ideas of what God was like were, as McKenzie pointed out, higher than the best pagan concepts. For the Greeks, for instance, "the gods of the ancient world were supermen and superwomen who had the freedom to behave like children." Yet one of the pictures that the Old Testament had of God was that of what McKenzie calls "Yahweh the Great Kinsman." "It is . . . surprising that modern Christians can so easily use the religious language of a tribal society without choking on it. This language is far more natural in the Mafia than it is in the republic of the United States of America, in which Uncle Sam is no Godfather." Throughout the Old Testament period pictures of God changed from regarding him as the Great Kinsman, the Feudal Overlord, the Righteous Judge, the Betrayed Lover, and the Cosmic Lord. As McKenzie said, "the image of God is determined by the humanity of the people who worship the God." This is not to say that "the humanity of God grows with the humanity of man." It is to say instead that as man remains in communication with God, his humanity grows, and thus his ability to recognize the greatness of God, his capacity to see in God qualities that were always there but which previously man did not have the experience to recognize or appreciate.[2]

Now I think that Father McKenzie's implication that some change in religion is a good thing can also be seen in our gospel for today. The passage is the one that always seems so unfair, the one about the man who hired farm workers all through the day from about sun-up to the last hour before quitting time and then paid all of them the same wage for that day's work. Of course the effectiveness of the parable depends on the appearance of unfairness. When the charge is made, the owner can point out that nobody was cheated. Even those who worked all day got the full union scale without even Cesar Chavez there to help them. They were well paid and had nothing to complain about. The only problem was that the owner had been only fair with them while he had been generous with the others. But everyone has to recognize that being generous is a good thing, even when we ourselves are not the beneficiaries of that generosity.

The point of that parable in the original preaching of Jesus was in relation to Jesus' warm acceptance of sinners. The pillars of the church and society, the Pharisees, thought that they were much more deserving of his attention than all of these dregs of society. Jesus' answer says in effect "Yeah, you've got a point. But you don't really have anything to complain about. You will get from God everything that you have coming to you. So why get upset if God wants to be generous with someone else?"

The point about change comes in here. Jesus changed the group of people who could be thought to be religious; he changed men's minds about what sort of people God cared for. He said that the Father was just as interested in ordinary folks as he was in pious people. And this change thing gets carried a little farther in our gospel for the day. It ends up with the saying that the last shall be first and the first shall be last. Biblical scholars are convinced that this line did not come from Jesus but from St. Matthew. The reason that Matthew put it in was apparently that he no longer knew about the struggle Jesus had with the Pharisees and so he didn't really understand the parable and he had to guess at its meaning and this is what he came up with. What he is referring to is not a distinction between Pharisees and ordinary Jews, but between Jews and gentiles. The people who followed God first, the Jews, had rejected Jesus and so they would be last. But the last people to learn about God, the gentiles, had accepted Jesus and they would now be first. So here again the meaning of the parable focuses on a change of the people that God cares for.

I think we can see from all this that it is true that some change in religion is for the better; not all, but some. And that change did not cease with the coming of Jesus, even though we do talk about the perfect revelation of the Father in and by the Son, and we speak the truth in saying so. There is a sense in which the faith was "once delivered to the saints" but there is also a sense in which what Cardinal Newman called the "development of doctrine" not only exists but is also valid. A few examples: the earliest Christians did not expect the Church to spread through the world because they expected Jesus to have his second coming before the first generation of Christians died out. When that belief changed, it was for the better. It was not until the early third century that the threefold ministry of bishops, priests, and deacons was completely established. It was not until the end of the fourth century that it was recognized exactly which books made up the New Testament. It was only with the Council of Nicea in 325 AD that the Church began really to see that Jesus is not only as much God as the Father, but that he is the same God as the Father. The relation of Jesus' human nature to his divine nature was not really understood until the fourth and fifth ecumenical councils in 451 and 553. And, to bring this up to date, it appears not to have been realized by anyone that slavery is immoral before the time of the American Revolution. From the abolitionist movement grew the whole concept of Christian social ethics that has been so much a part of Christian witness in this century. Another tremendous step forward in theology was the beginning of the modern historical and critical interpretation of the Bible. These changes have all taken place since Jesus ascended into heaven and they have all been improvements in Christianity. I think, then, that we are compelled to admit that not all change in the Church is bad.

Do-It-Yourself—A

The Third Sunday in Lent, 1972
Trinity, Wauwatosa
Gospel A

The technique for Do-It-Yourself sermons is that the preacher himself must have discovered some common principle operating between the "exhibits" that he offers and that the congregation must be left to discover this principle for themselves. In what follows, that common principle was the efforts of people to impose on one person their convictions about who he is or should be. Thus there is the ideal of the astronaut imposed on Aldrin, the ideal of the rock star imposed on Dylan, the ideal of a Jewish Messiah imposed on Jesus, the ideal of a wife imposed on the woman playing bridge, and the ideal of a child imposed on the boy with long hair. While the congregation may not see the same thing that the preacher did, quite often they may see more. This is a good way to get their psyches working for you.

The first exhibit comes from the *Milwaukee Journal*, February 27, 1972. It is a news story headlined, "Moon Trip Glamor Ended With Splashdown: Aldrin."

Carl Jung, the brilliant explorer of psychology, once remarked that "space flights are merely an escape, a fleeing away from oneself, because it is easier to go to Mars or to the moon than it is to penetrate one's own being."

Edwin (Buzz) Aldrin Jr., a scientific explorer himself and the second man to step on the moon, found Jung's remark in a newspaper not long ago and said somewhat ruefully: "If he only knew the whole story."

For Aldrin, the peculiar hazards of being an American hero began in July, 1969, when Apollo 11 splashed down in the Pacific. The splashdown, for Aldrin, was the beginning of another odyssey that led him out of the US space program and out of the Air Force, where he had spent all of his adult life.

Aldrin's partners on man's first moon landing have faded from the public's eye.

Neil Armstrong, the first man on the moon, has left the space program and now leads a life of relative obscurity as a professor at the University of Cincinnati.

Michael Collins, who stayed in the command ship, briefly joined the US State Department and now is an executive at the Smithsonian Institution.

Aldrin left NASA almost a year ago and returned to the Air Force as commandant of the Aerospace Research Pilot School at Edwards Air Force Base, Calif.

"I speak for myself, of course, but I think the others would agree that everything was fine until splashdown," Aldrin said. "We had been so busy preparing to go to the moon that we were unprepared for the impact the trip would have on our lives."

Aldrin speaks of his decade as an astronaut without rancor or bitterness and candidly admits that he would do it all over again. But when he contemplates the experience, it is almost with a sense of wonderment that he got through it at all.

"I remember one day picking up a copy of *Life* magazine with a story on us in it," Aldrin said. "We had a contract with *Life* and they owned the rights to our personal stories during the flights and the stories about our families. I remember reading the story and thinking, 'If only it was really like that.' Here were all the happy contented wives and children smiling out from happy back yards with husbands standing proudly by.

"Well, the fact is that the husband probably flew halfway

across the country to pose for the picture, the kids were half strangers to him and the wife was scared to death about any number of things. We were portrayed as perfect all-American people.

"Well, all-American maybe, but not perfect. There's no such thing. We had problems just as everyone does. The pressure to excel, to accomplish, was intense. So was the wear and tear of internal politics and rivalry. Feuds existed in the space program just as they do everywhere."

After he returned from the moon, Aldrin underwent psychiatric treatment for a month because "the whole thing gradually got to be too much."

"It has been kept somewhat of a secret, but the fact of the matter is that I was on my way to having a good old American nervous breakdown," Aldrin said. "I realized it and asked for help. I needed a long stop to look inside myself.

"There is a sort of stigma attached to mental illness of any sort and because so much was at stake—for the space program, the Air Force, myself and my family—it was kept secret. I no longer agree. Maybe I can give some person somewhere the courage to face his problems by saying something about mine.

"Astronauts are chosen for a number of reasons, but a major factor is our stability. We've got to be rock solid in the head. But what's happened to me can happen to anyone. Can and does. It sounds like a cliche, but I'm a much better man for my down and up experiences."

Shortly after he became commandant of the aerospace school at Edwards, Aldrin says he "just sort of gradually unwound."

"I knew I was sick, so I went to various doctors and my commanding officer and told them I wanted psychiatric help. I was sent to Wilford Hall, an Air Force hospital in San Antonio. People were informed an old neck injury put me in the hospital. This was only partially true."

Aldrin will retire from the Air Force March 1, earlier than previously announced. He plans to spend about three months—until his three children finish school—at his home in Edwards, and then do some traveling.

Aldrin is retiring as a full colonel, but his decision to quit was made before he had been passed over a second time for promotion to brigadier general. He publicly has stated that he is leaving the Air Force "with regret," but that his 10 years away from the service and its ways made catching up nearly impossible.

One can speculate on the reasons why he was not promoted, and one guess is that his brief bout with mental illness blemished his chances.

Mention this to Aldrin and he will smile pleasantly and say:

"I'm leaving that until later. The Air Force has been my life so far and I cannot really speak up—yet. What I've already said will cause enough comment.

"I'm writing a book. It is about my personal experiences as a man and an astronaut. I plan to say a lot of things in it. What I felt about returning from the moon plus some candid comments about NASA, politics and all the other things we became involved in. I'll tell you for sure it won't be like the old stories in *Life* magazine.

"The three of us in Apollo 11—with help, of course—wrote a book called 'First on the Moon.' My share of it last year amounted to $478. I suppose that's what you get for not telling it just like it was."

The second exhibit is Pierre-Rene Noth's column, "Sounds of the Times," in the *Milwaukee Journal.*

Bob Dylan is a legend, and legends never stand up well under close examination. Such a close examination is the just released *Bob Dylan: An Intimate Biography* by Anthony Scaduto (Grosset and Dunlap, $7.95). In it Dylan becomes more of a man and much less of a god.

Scaduto is a former police reporter and it shows in the way he has ferreted out the facts, sifted the lies from the truth and come up with a story that is more real than its participants—especially Dylan—might like.

Dylan has never appreciated his deification by music fans, but these 274 pages display him as far less of an ideal idol for the young than even his detractors imagined. He also comes across as human, for it is humans and not gods who are imperfect.

Scaduto has written perhaps the finest biography of Dylan

possible when denied intimate access to the source—although that may be an advantage because the book's digging reveals that one Dylan trait is the fabrication and embellishment of happenings in his life. It should also be considered volume one of a biography, for Dylan is only 30 and still has a lot of living and singing to do.

The portrait of the man is fascinating, puzzling. Scaduto traces the fibs, Dylan's male chauvinist use of women and winning women, his sitting as a disciple at the feet of Woody Guthrie, his romance with Joan Baez, his hunger for success and his arrogance in it, his retreat from an audience and world that wanted too much from him and too much of him.

It is a critical biography but not an unsympathetic one, for it makes clear the influences and background that caused Dylan to do some of the surprising things that he did—and to sing some of the surprising songs that he did.

Scaduto's biography is as exciting and mesmerizing as its topic.

Part of today's gospel and a little beyond it:

Then they took the man who had been blind to the Pharisees. The day that Jesus made the mud and opened the man's eyes was a Sabbath. The Pharisees, then, asked the man again how he had received his sight. He told them, "He put some mud on my eyes, I washed my face, and now I can see." Some of the Pharisees said, "The man who did this cannot be from God because he does not obey the Sabbath law." Others, however, said, "How could a man who is a sinner do such mighty works as these?" And there was a division among them. . . . A second time they called back the man that had been born blind and said to him, "Promise before God that you will tell the truth! We know that this man is a sinner." "I do not know if he is a sinner or not," the man replied. "One thing I do know: I was blind, and now I see." "What did he do to you?" they asked. "How did he open your eyes?" "I have already told you," he answered, "and you would not listen. Why do you want to hear it again? Maybe you, too, would like to be his disciples?" They cursed him and said: "You are that fellow's disciple; we are Moses' disciples. We know that God spoke to Moses; as for that fellow, we do not even know where he comes from!" The man answered, "What a strange thing this is! You do not know where he comes from, but he opened my eyes! We know that God does not listen to sinners; he does listen to people who respect him and do what he wants them to do. Since the beginning of the world it has never been heard of that someone opened the eyes of a man born blind; unless this man came from God, he would not be able to do such a thing." They answered back, "You were born and raised in sin—and you are trying to teach us?" And they threw him out of the synagogue.

Exhibit four:

It was a miserable evening of bridge. My wife and I do not play well or often. The husband in the other couple regarded himself as a pro. After each hand he would go back over the bidding and every trick and point out to his wife how stupidly she had played. While play was going on he advanced opinions about a variety of topics, always in a most authoritative voice; when his wife made a tentative foray into the conversation he swooped down on her verbally and showed that her contribution indicated ignorance of many facts and faulty reasoning about the ones she possessed. Between times there were opportunities to criticize her taste in clothing, her management of household finances, her family, her education, her social graces, and everything about her except her luck in finding a husband.

And finally:

The teen-aged boy is in the psychiatric ward of the hospital now. He will probably be there for at least six weeks. During the night while he was asleep his parents crept into his bedroom and cut off the long hair that they despised.

11

Do-It-Yourself—B

The Second Sunday in Advent, 1971
Trinity, Wauwatosa
Gospel A

This second example of the Do-It-Yourself sermon is based on the New Testament understanding that one is judged not so much by someone standing outside him and evaluating his actions, as by his own response to what happens. One is judged, for instance, by the way that he responds to messianic claimants and similar such things, whether they be modern persons claiming to be John the Baptist, John the Baptist himself, Jesus People, or a young girl whose murder could be prevented by the intervention of a person who cared.

When I was a pale young curate in Baton Rouge I was also in charge of a mission across the river in Port Allen. In those days the only bridge across the river was well north of town and it took no more time or money to get to the other side by a ferry that docked roughly where Main Street met the river. It was also much less hectic to cross that way and much more picturesque. The ferry did not have a paddle wheel although it looked like it ought to and there was something evocative of moonlight and magnolias about crossing the Father of Waters at a point where you could stand on deck and gaze at the state capitol. The romance of the crossing was invariably increased by the presence at the landing on the Baton Rouge side of an old black man that everyone called John the Baptist. I don't know whether he actually thought that he was John the Baptist or not, but whatever self image he did have was not a great deal less bizarre. He wore a white robe and had some sort of white covering on his head and carried a combination cross and staff that was made by tying two limbs of a sapling together and wrapping them in strips torn from an old sheet. He preached to all of the people who were parked waiting for the ferry to come but we never knew exactly what he was saying, because he mumbled a good deal. The only clear words I remember hearing him say were a thank-you to anyone who gave him money. I do believe that I witnessed a river baptism he was conducting once, but the catechumens appeared to have been recruited in the Negro quarter in which he lived rather than from those to whom he preached at the ferry stop. The community had an affectionate tolerance for him, probably because he was black and harmless and no one ever thought of having him locked up. According to my source of information on psychological matters he was probably mildly schizophrenic and suffered hallucinations but was never forced to a psychotic break because the community in which he lived was able to allow him to go his way without imposing unbearable restraints on him.

The gospel for the day tells of the original John the Baptist who must have appeared to his contemporaries to have a similar benign psychopathy if they had had the vocabulary in which to describe him. The area in which he operated is described as the desert or wilderness of Judea. This is the area in which the Judean mountains overlook the junction of the Jordan river and the Dead Sea. Jerusalem, a dozen miles away, has about the elevation of

Asheville, N.C., but the Dead Sea lies in a geological fault and is over 1200 feet below sea level. As one descends, he notices vegetation decrease to the point where it becomes non-existent and at the bottom, the lowest spot on the face of the earth, the landscape is lunar both in its ruggedness and in its barrenness. It was in this eerie area that John conducted his mission. He must have looked about as wild as the country. The camel's hair garment that he wore was not a polo coat, nor was it of hide, as it is usually depicted in church art, but was probably a rough cloth not very different from that out of which the Bedouins did and do construct their tents. A leather thong confined it at the waist. John's diet was what could be garnered in his desolate environment, locusts and wild honey. The locusts consisted of 75% protein, 3.4% fats and 7.5% carbohydrates. He told the people who came to hear him that somebody more important than he was coming, someone whose sandle laces he was not worthy to untie, and that man would separate people the way that a farmer separates wheat from chaff with a winnowing fork.

The odd thing is that John attracted huge crowds even though they had to make a difficult journey to get to where he was preaching. We learn of the success of his mission not only in the New Testament but also in the work of the Jewish historian, Josephus, who had nothing to gain by flattering the Christians. He tells of why King Herod Antipas had him executed:

Herod, who feared lest the great influence John had over the people might put it into his power and inclination to raise a rebellion (for they seemed ready to do anything he should advise) thought it best to put him to death to prevent any mischief he might cause.[1]

You are walking along Wisconsin Avenue and two young people come up to you. They are dressed about alike in blue jeans, Army surplus, and long untidy hair, but by intuition you know that one is male and the other female. You wonder what they want, feeling a little uneasy. Are they going to try to sell you narcotics or a copy of *Kaleidoscope*?* Are they going to ask for a handout? Or maybe they are going to mug you right there in broad daylight. It is with some astonishment that you hear their question: Are you saved? And then they begin to tell you about Jesus. You keep walking, pretending that you do not hear, understand, or care, but they walk along with you, one on each side, leaning in front of you to look into your eyes, and you feel pinned down by two machine guns that spout Bible verses instead of bullets, holding you in their withering crossfire. You are embarrassed and hope no one you know is watching and pray that they soon will give up on you and move on to another victim.

And last, from the *Milwaukee Journal* of November 28, 1971, comes a story headlined, "World Passed Slain Girl By."

Evening rush hour traffic streamed out of downtown Rochester. On the outskirts of the business district, cars and trucks swung onto four lane Interstate 490 and picked up speed.

They followed the curling highway through the pleasant suburb of Chili with its modern homes of pastel pink and blue, then hurried southwest through gently rolling farmland toward the New York State Thruway.

It was 5:30 p.m. on Tuesday, November 16. For most of the motorists, it was the end of another routine day at the office or plant.

Then something happened that made that day different from all other days.

As the cars bore down in the Route 36 interchange, a little girl suddenly appeared out of the darkness along the shoulder of the road.

She was naked, or nearly so, and some witnesses said she was

* An underground newspaper published in Milwaukee at the time.

waving as if trying to hail passing cars. They also noticed an auto along the shoulder of the road, backing toward the girl.

Police now believe that what the drivers saw was possibly the last desperate plea for help by Carmen Colon, 10, a petite Puerto Rican child who had been abducted from her Rochester neighborhood only an hour before. Police theorized that she momentarily escaped somehow from her abductor in the car along the shoulder in a frantic break for safety.

But nobody stopped, and two days later, almost at the same hour of the day, Carmen's body was found in a ditch in a remote section two miles away. An autopsy showed that she had been raped and strangled.

Why didn't one of the hundreds of motorists who passed the girl stop to help her?

"I couldn't believe what I saw," one motorist said, explaining his own reaction.

Another driver said he thought the girl had been let out of the auto "to go to the bathroom."

A third driver said he thought about going back to investigate, mentioned it to a passenger, but changed his mind.

"I felt someone behind was in a better position," he said.

"I was in the passing lane going 65 to 70 and there were five or six cars right behind me. I didn't expect it was anything sinister."

The reactions bear out much of the research done by Victor Harris, a social psychologist at the State University of Buffalo.

Harris, who has investigated so-called crowd apathy, said:

"There's a real question of whether, in fact, people even notice there's an emergency. They may see something going on, but not at a conscious level.

"Then they read about it in a paper later and say to themselves: 'Oh, that's what I saw happening the other day. My God! Something should have been done!' "

The drivers who passed the girl, he said, "may have been half concentrating on their driving and half concentrating on something else, like a business problem."

Even people who recognize what appears to be a desperate situation may not know how to cope with it, he said.

"An emergency is a rare occurrence to most people," Harris said. "They read a lot about them, but they seldom are confronted with them. Policemen and firemen are trained to react quickly to emergencies.

"If an offduty policeman had seen the child, he would have been more apt to react quickly to the situation and stop.

"Then again," Harris said, "there's the question: 'Should I help?' There's a belief in our society, you know, that everybody should mind his own business. It's a good idea in a way, but sometimes it can have bad consequences."

Michael Cerretto, chief sheriff's detective of Monroe County who heads the investigation into the slaying, is understanding.

"They were going 60 to 65," he said. "Some may have thought it was a family quarrel. What would you have done?

"Even now, some may feel if they come forward they would be ridiculed for failing to stop, but actually, it's understandable."

12

Preaching as Process

The Seventeenth Sunday after Pentecost, 1972
Trinity, Wauwatosa
Gospel A

The purpose of the Do-It-Yourself sermon is that the meaning not be imposed upon the hearer, but that he discover it for himself. What follows is an effort to help him do that. The general theme is that one does not really value values until they become the standard of his own life. The theme is almost Robert Bellah's statement: "Revolutionaries who in their own lives do not embody the future cannot bring it." [1] It begins with a ploy to show that gratitude is not just a matter of mouthing proper sentiments, but is in its fullest expression a happiness to use what was given. I tried to lead people into an awareness of this by representing various degrees of gratitude for a gift from one's wife. This was a real "back to the drawing board" sort of experience because no one got the point. We cannot generalize from this one particular and say that everyone has to flop every so often, but we can belabor the obvious and say that I do flop on regular occasions and that others may do the same. The other examples do not have to do with gratitude so much as forgiveness, but they do try to deal with our Lord's repeated statement that no one can be forgiven who does not accept forgiveness as his own way of life. The purpose of this sort of sermon is not to communicate propositions so much as it is to facilitate insight.

The other day my wife gave me a necktie and, after pointing out that it didn't match anything I owned, I went on to say that I would not wear a tie of that pattern to a dogfight.

The other day my wife gave me a necktie and I thanked her graciously and then asked if she would mind if I exchanged it.

The other day my wife gave me a necktie and I thanked her profusely and hung it on the back of the rack so that it would never be in the way when I was choosing a tie to wear.

The other day my wife gave me a necktie for which I thanked her and I made certain that I wore it once during the following week before I placed it on the back of the rack where it would not be in the way.

The other day my wife gave me a necktie that goes well with my blue suit and I wear it every once in a while.

The other day my wife gave me a necktie that was really rather nice and I wear it fairly often.

The other day my wife gave me a necktie and I liked it so well that I have hardly had it off since she gave it to me.

The other day my wife gave me a necktie and it was so beautiful that I not only wear it all the time, but I even went out and bought five more just like it: one for each of our sons, one for her father and one for mine, and one for the rector to wear on his day off.

Matt. 18:21–35: Then Peter came to Jesus and asked, "Lord, how many times can my brother sin against me and I have to forgive him? Seven times?" "No, not seven times," answered Jesus, "but seventy times seven. Because the Kingdom of heaven is like a king who decided to check on his servants' accounts. He had just begun to do so when one of them was brought in who owed him millions of dollars. He did not have enough to pay his debt, so his master ordered him to be sold as a slave, with his wife and his children and all that he had, in order to pay the debt. The servant fell on his knees before his master. 'Be patient with me,' he begged, 'and I will pay you everything!' The master felt sorry for him, so he forgave him the debt and let him go.

"The man went out and met one of his fellow servants who owed him a few dollars. He grabbed him and started choking him. 'Pay back what you owe me!' he said. His fellow servant fell down and begged him, 'Be patient with me and I will pay you back!' But he would not; instead, he had him thrown into jail until he should pay the debt. When the other servants saw what had happened they were very upset, and went to their master and told him everything. So the master called the servant in. 'You worthless slave!' he said. 'I forgave you the whole amount you owed me, just because you asked me to. You should have had mercy on your fellow servant, just as I had mercy on you.' The master was very angry, and he sent the servant to jail to be punished until he should pay back the whole amount." And Jesus concluded, "That is how my Father in heaven will treat you if you do not forgive your brother, every one of you, from your heart."

A scene from a modern Israeli novel, *Who? Me?* by Yoram Matmor. The incident takes place at the beginning of the Six Day War.

A few miles beyond the town, where the black tents of a Bedouin encampment squatted low on a hillside, the Military Police had thrown up a barrier on the road. The sergeant in charge was arguing with an old man dressed in khaki pants and a white shirt, whose square laborer's hands were holding on to a decrepit bicycle.

"You can't go up to the encampment without a permit," the sergeant was saying. "Martial law has been declared in the whole area."

"But I go up there every week," objected the old man. "We don't do anything—we just sit around and talk a little . . ."

The MP sighed. "There's a war on with the Arabs—or haven't you heard?"

The old man nodded vigorously. "That is why I came today—to show them that in spite of everything we're not . . ." He stopped, looking for words to express himself. The MPs looked at him with a cold, distant curiosity, as if he were an artifact exhibited in a small museum. I prodded the Professor in the back. "Tell them to let the old man go up," I whispered in his ear. He hesitated for a moment, probably on the point of telling me to mind my own business, then dipped his hand into his coat pocket, drew out his identity card, shoved it under the sergeant's nose, and said, "Let the old man go wherever he wants to, sergeant." The sergeant looked at the card, said, "Yes, sir," and said admonishingly, "You can go—but behave yourself!" The old man nodded to us lightly, as if we had done the only right thing to do, and walked up the hill pushing his bike.

The sergeant looked after him and shook his head. "I don't know what it is that makes them love the Arabs . . ."

"He has a very good reason," I said. "They murdered his daughter." There was a short silence; then the sergeant lifted the barrier, and we were off.

After about ten minutes the Professor asked, without turning toward me, "David—did the Arabs really kill his daughter?"

"They did," I answered. "She was working in a kibbutz near the border, herding sheep. One day they caught her alone in the fields and cut her to bits. Probably raped her, too." We traveled on and I was thinking about the old man and how, instead of hating and looking for revenge, he had decided to try friendship and understanding, because this was the only way he saw of saving someone's child, anybody's child.[2]

13

Non-directive Approach
to a Social Problem

A good deal of preaching on social problems has fallen short of its goal of converting the unpersuaded because its prophetic stance seems to place the preacher in an adversary relation to the congregation. The Do-It-Yourself technique does not draw conclusions, but leaves the congregation to do that. It is much easier to get mad at the minister than it is to become angry with the conclusions of one's own thought. Thus this method may open people to the Church's social responsibility in a way that direct confrontation may not.

Thanksgiving at our house was quite an occasion. I report on ours, not because I think that it was unusual, but because I imagine it was typical. We had a number of friends over since family were all too far away to come. There were twenty-two of us in all. Dinner was quite a production. For hors d'oeuvres with our sherry we had devilled eggs and a dieter's delight of cut-up celery, carrot sticks, and cauliflower to dip with. The meal itself centered around a twenty-three pound turkey and a new kind of dressing that had apples, raisins, and nuts in it. There was, of course, gravy to pour over all that. Vegetables included broccoli with a cheese sauce and yams with marshmallows. There was a cranberry and orange salad as well as plain old cranberry sauce for those with traditional taste. There were buttered rolls, both Parker House and whole wheat. To wash it all down there was rosé. For dessert one could choose between pecan, mince, and pumpkin pie or plum pudding. And naturally there was coffee.

It was just ten years ago that Michael Harrington alerted us all to the problem of poverty in this country by writing his book, *The Other America.* Two years later in his State of the Union address President Johnson declared a war on poverty. While Harrington had estimated that 40,000,000 American people were impoverished, the President pointed out that the per capita income of 35,000,000 had been $590, compared to the national average of $1,900. At the time this amounted to 22% of our population. To an extent the war on poverty was successful: According to the Census Bureau, only 13% of the population was impoverished in 1968. Since that time, though, the improvement has ceased. We have levelled off to where most authorities recognize that between ten and fifteen per cent of our people live below the governmentally established poverty line. That line was defined in 1971 as an annual income of $4,137 for an urban family of four. Roughly one out of eight of our citizens lives in "the other America."

Then he shall say to those on his left, 'Away from me, you that are under God's curse! Away to the eternal fire which has been prepared for the Devil and his angels! I was hungry but you would not feed me, thirsty but you would not give me drink; I was a stranger but you would not welcome me in your homes, naked but you would not clothe me; I was sick and in prison but you would not take care of me.' Then they will answer him, 'When, Lord, did we ever see you hungry, or thirsty, or a stranger, or naked, or sick, or in prison, and we would not help you?' The King will answer them back, 'I tell you, indeed, whenever you refused to help one of these least important ones, you refused to help me.' These, then, will be sent off to eternal punishment; the righteous will go to eternal life.

The current issue of *Psychology Today* includes a report on a survey taken recently to determine the attitudes of Americans toward their fellow Americans who are impoverished. When they were asked what they thought the reasons were that some people are impoverished, 58% of those questioned said that a very important reason is a lack of thrift and proper money management. 55% saw a lack of effort by the poor people themselves as a very important factor, while 52% so rated a lack of ability and talent among the poor. 48% believed that loose morals and drunkenness were significant. Against these individualistic explanations, which say in effect that it is the fault of the poor themselves that they are poor, explanations which tended to blame the system were much less frequently given. Only 36%, for instance, saw poor education as a very important factor, only 33% thought racial prejudice was largely responsible, and merely 27% blamed industry for not supplying enough jobs. A bare 18% said that the poor are being taken advantage of by the rich. When the explanation moved from blaming it on the individual and blaming it on the system to putting it down as just bad luck, only 8% of those questioned made this fatalistic interpretation.

Not surprisingly, there was a high correlation between explanations of why people were poor and attitudes toward welfare. People who blame the poor for their own condition are likely to think that there are too many people receiving welfare who should be working, that some people on welfare are not honest about their needs, that some mothers on welfare have more children to increase their payments, and that a lot of people are moving into this state from other states just to get welfare money here. Some of these opinions, incidentally, have been conclusively disproved. 80% of the illegitimate children born in this country do not receive welfare, less than a third of the children on welfare are illegitimate, and in Utah, at any rate, 90% of the illegitimate children on welfare were born before their parents were on welfare.

There is also a high correlation between blaming the poor for their own poverty, opposing welfare, and opposing either guaranteed jobs that are supported by taxes or opposing guaranteed annual income. Joe R. Feagin, who directed the research and wrote the article, has concluded:

As long as large numbers of Americans attribute social problems to character defects of individuals, massive economic reform will be extraordinarily difficult. Individualistic interpretations of poverty mesh well with conservative attempts to maintain the status quo. Indeed, major improvements in the American economy . . . may require—among other things—a major shift in American attitudes and values.[1]

A poem by Bob Rowland:

    Listen Christian

            I was hungry and you formed a humanities club and discussed my hunger. Thank you.

            I was imprisoned and you crept off quietly to your chapel in the cellar and prayed for my release.

            I was naked, and in your mind you debated the morality of my appearance.

            I was sick and you knelt and thanked God for your health.

I was homeless and you preached to me of the spiritual shelter of the love of God.

I was lonely and you left me alone to pray for me.

You seem so holy; so close to God. But I'm still very hungry, and lonely and cold.

Thank you, thank you, thank you.[2]

14

Forming Central Beliefs

The Seventh Sunday of Easter, 1973
Trinity, Wauwatosa
Gospel B

As Welsh has said, "Clearly the closed mind is highly
resistant to direct argument. Even the exposition of
contradictions within its belief system does not produce
modifications within it, for the closed mind is not logically
but psychologically structured." [1] *In order not to threaten*
people who have closed minds, Welsh suggests that the
preacher should avoid abstract summary statements and
approach the matter instead through concrete life situa-
tions that at first appear to be neutral with regard to the
subject under discussion. The closed mind is in its most
closed state when dealing with central beliefs that repre-
sent a fundamental stance toward life. The sermon that
follows is an effort to deal with a closed mind that takes a
pessimistic view of the world, the sort of view that most
such minds take, as Welsh tells us. It tries to do so by
acknowledging at the beginning and through concrete
data that there is much to be said for that position, but
goes on to offer other data that is non-confrontational,
but which nevertheless argues to a different conclusion. I
have thus used the principle of "interlocking" that

Linnemann tells us is characteristic of Jesus' parables (see p. 51).

This morning we are going to have some more clippings from my file, but this time the connection between them will be quite explicit. First, this news story from the current *Newsweek*, entitled "The Year of the Famine."

Across the face of India last week, angry mobs were on the march. In Agra, they looted grain shops. In Bombay, they smashed the cars of the rich. In Limdi, they plundered a government warehouse. And in the town of Tumsar, they stormed the home of a local politician, seized tons of rice and cattle feed that he had been hoarding and stoned to death a policeman who tried to stop them—dragging his body through the streets in a ghoulish parade of triumph. The desperate savagery of the Indian rioters was born of hunger. Their land parched by drought, their crops dead and their cattle dying, some 200 million Indians face the threat of a disastrous famine in the months ahead.

The looming catastrophe is not confined to India. A tragic mixture of drought and crop-destroying floods has crippled rice production in a number of Southeast Asian nations ranging from Bangladesh and Sri Lanka (formerly Ceylon) all the way to the Philippines. In China, which has just begun to produce enough to feed its 800 million people, an estimated 40 million are confronting the grim prospect of hungry months ahead.

The situation in Africa is even worse. The most severe drought in 60 years has turned vast portions of six impoverished West African countries—Mauritania, Senegal, Mali, Upper Volta, Niger and Chad—into arid wastelands. "If the problem is not solved in two months," warns Mourtada Diallo, a regional director of the United Nations Economic Commission for Africa, "nearly 6 million people may die."

The crisis has already begun to take its toll, not so much in human lives—although thousands have died—but in the destruction of the land and the deaths of livestock. The worst is yet to come. According to the European Common Market's

Commissioner of Agriculture Pierre Lardinois, the afflicted West African region faces "a disaster of a magnitude which we still cannot measure in all its consequences." And in India, some states are confronted by what one expert has called the "worst famine in living memory." Tragically, not even a good rainfall, which still might come in the next month or two, may be enough to avert a calamity. Human greed and corruption have kept food and water from a number of the neediest areas. What's more, the myopic pride of some of the governments involved, which refuse even to acknowledge the potential catastrophe, has delayed imports of relief supplies so long that they may not be distributed in time.

The first warning signs of potential famine in India appeared last fall when the autumn harvest in the drought-prone regions fell nearly 60 per cent below expectations. Thousands of peasants began to flood the already overcrowded cities to beg for food. And in the countryside, the famous "green revolution" dried up along with the rivers and wells. While the government proclaimed that it was amassing a reserve food supply of 10 million tons, in fact the stores never topped half that amount. To make matters worse, India requires an additional 4 to 5 million tons of food per year just to meet the needs of its growing population. Attempts to draw New Delhi's attention to the mounting crisis were met with rebuff. Only recently, India's Foreign Ministry told journalists not to visit drought areas because, as an official put it, "we are sick and tired of these horror stories about India."

Rations: But the horror stories are true. In the hardest-hit areas, New Delhi has clamped severe rations on food, limiting each person to no more than 18 pounds per month—which is not enough to provide the number of calories considered necessary for the minimal "human survival level." Throughout the drought regions, half-starved Indians line up for hours in temperatures that range up to 116 degrees to receive their rations—but many leave empty-handed because of insufficient supplies. In a frenzied effort to combat the danger, the government has nationalized the food-grains trade and commandeered passenger trains to ship food into the affected areas. But the "food specials" have so far proved inadequate to meet the people's needs, and the attempts to bring all wholesale rice and wheat sales under government control have been sabotaged by the displaced wholesalers and farmers who have hidden away sizable portions of their supplies to sell on the burgeoning black market at inflated prices."

Similar reports are given of conditions and inappropriate governmental response in the rest of Asia, including China, and in Africa. The article concludes:

Relief is on the way to the stricken zones—the Common Market has pledged $20 million in aid, France has promised an additional $6 million and the U.S. is contributing some 156,000 tons of food. (In stark contrast, African nations have not committed any relief supplies to the area and, in fact, seem to be ignoring the problem completely.) But this latest food crisis is occurring at a time when once-massive agricultural surpluses elsewhere in the world—notably in the U.S.—are beginning to dwindle. And even the assistance that other areas can offer will not undo the damage that has been done. Drought has wrecked millions of acres of cultivated and grazing land—making it unusable for years to come. And as a result of protein deficiency, tens of thousands of children are destined to grow up as mental and physical cripples. "Perhaps the problem will be tackled by the richer nations of the world," says one pessimistic United Nations official based in Africa. "But it will take many years and if it is not started soon, it will already be too late for many future generations of Africans and Asians." [2]

Today is the Sunday after the Feast of the Ascension. It is possible to talk about the ascension as an historical event, but the theological significance of saying that Jesus ascended into heaven is that he now rules the universe. This is what we mean in the creed when we say that he sits at the right hand of the Father. But again, to be theologically significant, the statement that Jesus reigns has to be a statement not so much about Jesus in himself as it is a statement about the world. To say that Jesus reigns is to say that the world is ruled by him.

It is interesting to study the New Testament and trace the various stages of insight into the work of Christ that we find there. At first the Christian affirmation was merely that Jesus rose from the dead. But, since the early Church expected him to return soon, it also said, "Christ will come again." As long as his imminent return was expected, there was no reason to ask what he was doing in the meanwhile, but when it was realized that his return would not be soon, that question became necessary. The answer given is the affirmation that we are making today; he is sharing in his Father's rule of the universe. From this the Church went on to see that if Jesus shares in the reign of the Father, he must share in the Father's nature and so he must be eternal with the Father. This meant that he had existed from all eternity with the Father before his birth on earth. He had indeed participated with his Father in the creation of the universe.

Now a little lesson like this in the development of early Christian doctrine is interesting but it seems to have very little to say to us when we contemplate such an event as the famine that stretches from Africa to China. It is hard to think about that famine and say with much conviction that Jesus rules the universe. First there is the simple question of weather. If Jesus reigns and if God is love, why are there floods and why is there drought that leaves millions of people dying from lack of food? And how can we say that Jesus reigns when we see political officials who are too concerned with their own reputations and those of their countries to do anything about these conditions in their countries or even to admit that anything needs to be done? How can we say that Jesus reigns when profiteers are more interested in growing richer off the sale of scarce commodities than they are in the survival of their fellow countrymen? And how can we say that Jesus reigns when we read of the deaths of such large numbers of people and do nothing about it but discuss it in a Sunday School class?

Of course, the famine in Africa and Asia is one of many possible examples that might be cited. Watergate, for instance, is another experience that raises the question of whether Jesus reigns. And the futility and self-centeredness of my own life is another.

This morning I am not going to try to answer the question of how we can affirm that Jesus reigns with irrefutable logic, weighty evidence, and rational persuasion. Instead, I am going to place against the one experience of the world that the famine is, a couple of other sorts of experience. One is a poem that is written to speak of the inevitability of death, but what it says about the accomplishment of men who have lived tells me in a way that I cannot question that God's venture in creation was not wasted.

Consider me, I pray you

Consider me, I pray you. Consider that I—I, and no other—loved Helen and Io and Hecuba and created the Brandenburg concerti and the Oresteian trilogy and the Sistine ceiling and the pyramids that never perish.

Yes, and salted Carthage and buried Troy and burned Berlin and Indochina, and cut down continents and paved them, and planted my feet on the moon.

And installed another man's heart into a breathing man, and found the miracle drugs and the neutron and the secret of life in DNA.

Only consider, I pray you, and then judge between me and fleshless sneakthief Death, and tell me if I am to be done down by a shadow and become the dirt from which my marvelous carpetmakers with their deathless dyes protected my powdered and perfumed feet.

I tell you that I am Man and there is none like me.

I tell you that I will not take death lying down.[3]

So much for the goodness of creation. Now evidence for

the success of our Lord's redemptive activity. It comes from a book that one of you lent me. Last Christmas when we discussed the cover article in *Newsweek* about Paul Moore, the bishop of New York, one of you let me borrow a book his wife wrote about the eight years they spent in their first parish, and the work that they and their associates did there. That parish was Grace Church, Jersey City. The part I quote is her evaluation of their time spent in this pioneer work of the Episcopal Church in what we have now learned to refer to as the "inner core."

. . . there is more to Second Street than stair carpeting and vital statistics about our friends, more to our eight years there than nostalgia. Jersey City changed our lives, but how did we change our small part of Jersey City? What did we accomplish? What can be accomplished in a time of riots and calls for black separatism?

No one has to tell us that we didn't begin to change the system except to smooth some of its edges, and those impermanently. Although today there are more jobs available, more public housing, more telephones, cars, and better plumbing, the hard, cold, unassailable fact remains that the people on Second Street live outside that world that grows more affluent with every turn. They are still politically powerless, groggy from television's half-truths, patronized by handouts from a grossly inefficient welfare system. We changed none of that. But we did live there as a family; we were part of the community; we had no contract to fulfill. We didn't sign up for two years to work a block, and when there were parish projects we didn't calculate the amount of "feasible participation of the poor." We were never that efficient, and our criteria for evaluating our work were as vague as the facts of Harry's circus career.

We were neither a family guidance service nor social workers, although Bob, Kim, and Paul had had some counseling training in seminary. In an age of growing super-specialization, we were untutored generalists. Perhaps it would have been professional to give Mrs. Powell some ideas for a balanced diet realistic for her tiny pension, had I had that kind of knowledge. But we liked

Mrs. Powell, and we laughed with her. She was fun, and I have a feeling that it was her own sense of worth as a person, which our mutual enjoyment of one another helped keep alive, that sustained her. I know any grocery list I might have given her would have shot its way over the table (holding her Manhattan cocktail) in a rapidly constructed spitball. It might have been helpful to George, the El Greco bum, if we could have taught him to cane chairs, but I haven't a shadow of a doubt that it was more important that he had a home to visit on Second Street where no demands would be made, where no one would try to "improve" him. It could have proved constructive if we'd had more psychiatric help for many of the children who came around; it would certainly have been a help to have had more than one remedial reading teacher.

All those things might have improved the lot of our Jersey City friends, but they were not as important as our simply being *there*. Primarily—and leaving aside psychological motives from our own backgrounds—we lived on Second Street because we believed in God and in the unique worth of every person. The concept sometimes seemed either too simple or too complex— I've never known which—for daily certitude (there *were* mornings when we would wake up and wonder what we were doing there). Nonetheless, it overarched our lives like the Jersey City clotheslines. I believe it worked. I know that the boys who played ball in our yard and grew into the men who hate "Whitey" today remember the talks when they were in their teens around our kitchen table: about girls and sex, about being black, about Africa, about Jersey City politics. Even though they may hate "Whitey" now, I persist that to a man they could walk this moment into our house on the shady, tree-lined street in Washington and there would still be no barriers between us. And breaking down barriers is what I have been talking about.[4]

I don't know about you, but the mere fact that things like this can happen means to me that Jesus does indeed reign, that life makes sense, that it is all worth the effort. As the Prayer Book says, "Alleluia. Christ the Lord ascendeth into heaven. O come let us adore him. Alleluia."

The Content of the Sermon
Is What the Preacher Says Plus
All That the Congregation Hears

The Second Sunday of Easter, 1972
Trinity, Wauwatosa
Gospel A

All of our arguments for saying that what the preacher says is only a small part of the sermon make no difference unless some evidence can be offered. What follows is a sermon and the discussion that was a response to it. The discussion isolates at least some of the points at which the sermon touched personal concerns of the congregation. This particular discussion is included, not because it was the best that came in response to any of the sermons, but because it was the one that we were able to record best on the cassette player.

If you were to go to the Church of the Holy Sepulchre in Jerusalem you would see many wonderful things: Golgotha, the rock on top of which Jesus was crucified; the tomb of Jesus from which he rose; the underground cave where St. Helena, the mother of the Emperor Constantine, is said to have found the cross on which Jesus died; and a number of chapels and monasteries for Christian bodies from all over the world. There is one thing that you might easily overlook, though, and yet it is quite fascinating when your attention is called to it. In the middle of what we would call the nave of the church—about half way between the tomb and the high altar of the Greeks—is a small ceramic object about a foot and a half tall that is shaped roughly like a covered compote. It is called the *omphalos*, the Greek word for navel, and the theory behind it is that the Church of the Holy Sepulchre represents the navel of the universe; that is to say, it is the geometric center of the world. What it means to call any point on the surface of a sphere its center is questionable, but we know what is meant here. Since the most important events in the history of the world occurred on that spot, it is very appropriately called the center of the universe.

The trouble starts when you go a few short blocks away to the place where the Jewish Temple was from the time of Solomon until its final destruction forty years after the Resurrection. That area has been occupied by the Muslims since the seventh century. Shortly after they took over, they erected the most beautiful building I have ever seen over the spot where the altar of the Temple used to be. The place is holy for them, not only because they think that there Abraham would have sacrificed his son Isaac, but also because they believe that Mohammed ascended into heaven from there. And so the Muslim guide who shows you through will tell you that the rock over which it is built is the navel of the universe.

And when you go on to Greece to visit the great shrine of Apollo at Delphi, you can almost believe that the Delphic oracle did answer the questions of life that were presented there because no spot of natural beauty that you have ever seen testifies so much to the supernatural power that made it and seems to inhabit it. You are not surprised when you go through the magnificent museum there at Delphi and see a large stone hemisphere entwined with strange carvings; it is called the *omphalos* because of the legend that Zeus, father of the gods, released two eagles—one to fly east and the other west—and they met at Delphi, the center of the universe.

The great scholar of comparative religion, Mircea Eliade, tells us that considering one's own most holy place to be the center of the universe is one of the commonest features of world religions. Indeed, not only every altar, but even every household hearth is thought to be the center, so that centers are everywhere. Now that is a beautiful thought and we can all enjoy it—until we get around to the embarrassing implication. If centers are everywhere, then no place is more the center than another. The site of our Lord's death and resurrection is no more important than the Muslim Dome of the Rock at Jerusalem, the Temple of Apollo at Delphi, the medicine lodge of an Asiatic shaman, or the hearth of a Navajo hogan. If religions are equally true, then they are equally false.

This chilling relativism becomes even more frigid when we bring it into our neighborhood. Across the street is the Christian Science church and down the block the Congregationalists offer their worship. Not far away are Lutherans, Roman Catholics, and Greek Orothodox. From the yellow pages of the phone book I have gathered that there are Jewish synagogues at least near Wauwatosa and a Bahai temple within the city. With all of these flavors of public worship and many more being sampled within our community, the claim of the Prayer Book must sound rather astonishing: "Therefore with angels and archangels and all the company of heaven we laud and magnify thy glorious name." We say that what we do gathered around this one of many altars in Wauwatosa is to participate in the praise of the court of heaven offered to the Father. What we do here is of cosmic significance. Our little handful of people have a call on the attention of the Creator of the universe. Now that either means that we are doing something that all of the other congregations in this city are not doing or that they too are making contact; that centers are everywhere.

This almost comic incongruity between the exalted claims that we make for ourselves and our reality as it is seen from an earthly perspective is caught splendidly by C.S. Lewis when he has the archtempter Screwtape write to his nephew Wormwood about how to re-capture a soul that has lately been converted to Christianity:

All your patient sees [when he goes to church] is the half-finished, sham Gothic erection on the new building estate. When he goes inside, he sees the local grocer with rather an oily expression on his face bustling up to offer him one shiny little book containing a liturgy which neither of them understands, and one shabby little book containing corrupt texts of a number of religious lyrics, mostly bad, and in very small print. When he gets into his pew and looks around him he sees just that selection of his neighbors whom he has hitherto avoided. You want him to lean pretty heavily on those neighbors. Make his mind flit to and fro between an expression like "the body of Christ" and the actual faces in the next pew . . . Provided that any of those neighbors sing out of tune, or have boots that squeak, or double chins, or odd clothes, the patient will quite easily believe that their religion must therefore be somehow ridiculous.[1]

Screwtape could have learned all of these tricks in the trade of tempting from dealing with the Apostle Thomas in today's gospel. Thomas was not present at the first post-resurrection appearance of Jesus to the disciples reported by St. John. When the others told him that they had seen the Lord, he skeptically replied: "If I do not see the scars of the nails in his hands, and put my finger where the nails were, and my hand in his side, I will not believe." Well, within a week Thomas did get to be in on a "Show and Tell" session with the risen Lord and he kept his promise to believe under those circumstances, but we are told that his faith was not of the best sort. Jesus said to Thomas: "Do you believe because you see me? How happy are those who believe without seeing me!"

One of those happy people is included in the gospel, and it looks like St. John intended for us to see the contrast between him and Thomas. When Mary Magdalene told the disciples that Jesus' tomb was empty on Easter morning, two of them ran there to see what had happened. One of them was Peter, and the other is described mysteriously as "the other disciple whom Jesus loved."

The two of them were running, but the other disciple ran faster than Peter and reached the tomb first. He bent over and saw the linen cloths, but did not go in. Behind him came Simon Peter, and he went straight into the tomb. . . . Then the other disciple, who had reached the tomb first, also went in; he saw and believed. [They still did not understand the scripture which said that he must be raised from death.]

We don't know who this Beloved Disciple was. Traditionally he has been identified with St. John himself, but some scholars think that he represents the ideal disciple who is a model for all Christians ever afterwards. Certainly he was one of those happy ones, with faith superior to Thomas', who believed without seeing. And all of us who have come later in time have also had to believe without seeing. But the real point is that the Beloved Disciple's belief without sight was more accurate than Thomas' belief with sight. He knew when he first went into the tomb of Jesus that it was the *omphalos*, the center of the universe.

And there is another book in the New Testament which shows us something of what that accurate kind of belief can do. The book was written either by this same St. John or, more likely, by a member of his theological school. It is the Revelation that was written to inspire Christians on the western coast of Turkey when they were in danger of being persecuted for their refusal to worship the Roman emperor instead of the Lord Jesus. This inspiring word is set in the context of heavenly worship just as our Eucharist is. The message that came through was that the mighty Roman empire was going to perish but the Church would last forever. Who could have believed it then? Rome had conquered the civilized world of that time, and the captive people on the Aegean, far from despising their conquerors, worshipped Caesar as a god for bringing them peace and prosperity. The Church at the time amounted to no more than a handful of people in seven cities along the coast; they must have looked pretty weird to their contemporaries. When they said that Christ was mightier than Caesar, they must have sounded like they had delusions of grandeur. But in less than 300 years, their religion was made the only legal religion in the empire and the empire was in danger of cracking up and clung to the Church as the only glue strong enough to hold it together. John was right in his faith without vision and all the people round about were wrong when they trusted the evidence of their eyes. It was not Rome that was eternal but the Church. The tomb was the *omphalos*.

And when we come into Trinity Church, Wauwatosa, on this Second Sunday of Easter, where grocery men pass out hymn books, shoes squeak, and some people sing off key, we too can distrust the evidence of our eyes and say, "Therefore with angels and archangels and with all the company of heaven, we laud and magnify thy glorious name."

DISCUSSION

Edwards. Okay, where does that put us? Probably in need of more coffee . . . . Good!

Parishioner. Well, maybe I misinterpret what you are saying. It raises a question in my mind that has been bothering me for some time. That is, if Christianity is all that hot, why doesn't this idea permeate and spread and really take over the entire world where, in fact, today I guess Christianity makes up less than a fourth of the religious people in the world? Why do people like the Buddhists and that sort of belief . . . do they get to heaven, or is Christianity the only answer?

E. H'm . . . . Well, what do you think?

P. I don't know. I'm asking you, really.

E. Well, does anyone else have . . . ?

P. We wouldn't be here if we didn't think this was the answer.

E. So the question is: Since Christianity hasn't really become the religion of the world, how are we to assume that Christianity is the only true religion? The answer that has been suggested is that we would not be here if we did not think that Christianity was the true religion. How does that grab you?

P. That's no answer. Lots of people supported Hitler; does that make them right? They were there because they believed Hitler, what he was trying to come up with.

E. Are you saying that the popular success of something is no indication of its truth?

P. That's exactly what I am saying.

E. But let me turn this back to our suggestion that we are here because we believe that Christianity is true. Now there are two different things going here, I think. One is the question of how you decide whether something is true or not, and the other is the question of what our presence in church indicates: That we may have a conviction that remains our conviction even if we are not able to demonstrate the truth of that conviction to the satisfaction of everyone else.

P. I think we are faced today with the situation in Ireland

where we have two groups of Christians who believe that
they are right so they use this as a springboard to cause
distress one upon another, all in the name of dear, sweet
Jesus. That shows you how far off (quote) Christians (close
quote) can be.

E. Good! This really does muddy up the water nicely. The
situation in Ireland where Christians are willing to shoot
one another in the name of Christ shows that sincerity is
not the final criterion of the truth of someone's belief. So
however sincerely we may believe that what we do is the
right thing, this does not prove that it is so. . . . Good!

P. Wouldn't it appear that one point going, one of the
things that bothers me personally, is faith? My faith
sometimes more often seems more like a negative thing
instead of a positive thing. It is difficult for me to believe
there isn't a God. It is difficult for me to believe that there
isn't a Hereafter. I end up coming from negativism instead
of positivism. Is this a common problem of a practicing
Christian today?

E. How much of a problem is it?

P. Some people tell me that it should be more positive.
You see, this means I must be wrong in my negative
approach. I take it from what people say that my approach
must therefore be wrong.

E. I'm wondering about the logical status of this, how the
content of what you call your negative faith differs from
the content of someone's positive faith. Because if someone says there is a God, there is eternal life, you say, "I
find this very hard to doubt." That's the negative way of
stating the same affirmation, but it is an affirmation that is
being made.

P. I think I agree with you, but the direction with me
seems to come from the negative side rather than the
positive, I believe.

E. Well, in the history of theology there is a very strong
tradition of what is called the *via negativa*, the negative

way, in which it is realized that in the final analysis God so exceeds the capacities of our language that no positive statement about him (with the possible exception of the statement that God exists) can be true in a literal sense. You can say that God is great, but what does it mean for God to be great? God is beyond all our distinctions. There has been quite a tradition of this negative way. I'm not sure but that you are in it and I'm not sure that is a bad thing . . . Yes?

P. Wouldn't you say that possibly when you look at religion in history more intellectually, wouldn't you be more likely to find your answer more by eliminating and thereby having negation rather than if your religion is emotional when you would have everything positive? But when you look at things intellectually, [what was said here was indistinct].

E. So we have a distinction posed between an intellectual religion and an emotional religion. An intellectual religion arrives at truth by negation, excluding alternatives, while an emotional religion is affirmative. I think, as an illustration of that, that St. Thomas Aquinas, in certainly one of the greatest intellectual presentations of the Christian faith that has ever been made, would make a statement, raise a question, then he would go through all kinds of objections to the statement first and then he would say, ". . . which is absurd, and therefore cannot be believed," or something like that and thereby eliminate each of the alternatives and then he'd say that what was left over had to be it. I wonder how much ultimately we want to press the distinction between intellectual and emotional religion because intellectuals, I think, among other things, feel very passionately about what their minds deal with, so that their emotions are involved there. And I can't imagine anyone whose religion was so emotional that it was deprived of any rational content . . . Yes?

P. I don't disagree with that, but I think that the gospel

for this morning fits precisely into this rubric, if I can use that term. Thomas needed the proof and Jesus said, "Happy are those who believe without the proof." And here is the example of the emotional contrasted with the rational.

E. Mr. ———— says that St. Thomas represents the intellectual sort who has to have everything proved to him and that, say, the Beloved Disciple would represent the emotional sort who can proceed on faith. But I wonder if that is quite the relation between faith and reason? Because one of the things we are saying here is that these two men had two different intellectual points of view. Each of them was offering a description of reality as he understood it, and we can't say that Thomas' was more intellectual and therefore more accurate. In fact, what we have said is that the Beloved Disciple's was a far more accurate description of reality than Thomas' was and we are not saying that it was emotion as such. I think we are saying that he was using a different kind of evidence.

P. I don't disagree with that, but I think you are drawing the wrong parallel. My parallel was with the statement of Christ, which I can't quote exactly from the gospel but was to the effect that, "Happy are those who believe without seeing." It was a blessing that the disciple did see. He came in and saw where Christ had laid and did believe. He had some evidence, but Jesus said, "Blessed are those who believe without seeing."

E. I think the point of the story in the gospel is that an empty tomb doesn't prove anything except that the body is not there. Because, remember, when I was reading from this passage, it went on immediately to say that they didn't yet understand that Jesus was supposed to rise. They had had nothing to precondition them to expect the resurrection and the category of resurrection had just not entered their minds before. Now, as a more natural response to this situation, we have Mary Magdalene coming along later and seeing Jesus and not even recognizing that it was Jesus, thinking he was the gardener and saying, "Where did you put the body?" You see, this is the . . . If I go into any grave and find it empty, I'm going to assume there have been some grave robbers around, that a medical school may need a few cadavers or something. I'm not going to assume that anybody has risen from the dead. Especially if nobody has done anything to suggest to me beforehand that there is going to be a resurrection from the dead. And now, there is some conflict here between the synoptic gospels and John. St. Mark, for instance, has three quite explicit predictions of the resurrection, but the disciples don't understand those. But John says there hadn't even been any such predictions and so when he gets there and he believes, I think that we are saying that he has a kind of spiritual insight that put him far beyond the evidence, that he was able to get there a great deal faster. Most New Testament scholars do believe that there is actually intended a parallel between his believing without seeing and Thomas' not believing until he did see, and that both of them, both of these stories, have very much in mind all of us who came along later and who never had the possibility of seeing the risen Lord. The only kind of faith that is possible for us is faith without sight, so when Jesus said, "Blessed are those who believe and do not see," he was talking not only about the Beloved Disciple, he was talking about all of us who come afterwards. We are the other sheep not of that fold that Jesus has.

Rector. It seems like what we have to deal with first is something John alluded to, the way people who believed in Hitler were wrong. I think there has been a fallacious proposition set forth particularly in the last twenty-five to fifty years, that it doesn't matter what you believe in as long as you believe in something. This is so wrong, because if I didn't believe that fire burned and put my fingers into it, I'd still get burned. If I didn't believe that the skull and

crossbones on a bottle meant exactly that it was poison-
ous, and took it, I would learn in a hurry. I think that we
have, in my way of thinking, to accept before we can go on
into any further depth. Christianity is unique or it isn't. Is
Jesus the Son of God or isn't he? If he is, then we have to
accept what the Bible says about him and what he said
about himself: "I am the resurrection and the life. He that
believeth in me, though he die, liveth eternally." Now if
Christianity is only one in amongst other religions, if it is
only one, then I would say, "Let's forget it!" We are only a
group of people meeting together as other people meet
together in their religions. If Christianity is unique, if Jesus
is the Son of God, if he was born in this world immacu-
lately, if all the things we say in the creed are true, then
indeed Christianity is unique and we had better heed our
Lord's words and go out and baptize and preach in the
name of him. Our commission is for all of us and not just
the apostles.

E. So, Father ———— is saying that when we come to this
kind of relativism, while we have to recognize the fact that
there are truth claims made by all religious groups, we
have to believe that the truth claims of Christians are
privileged. That is to say that when we say that what we
are saying is true, we are true in saying that it is true, and
this is very important. What we're saying is that a
statement is either true or false, whatever the moral
condition of the person who makes it. Jesus either did
reveal in a final way the nature of God, or he did not.
There is explicit objective content to that revelation or
there is not. Jesus rose or he didn't. Either God acted
decisively in Jesus for the reclamation of a lost world or he
did not. I think we would get less broad-minded about the
religious claims of various people if we start seeing how
Joe Smith as an engineer would want to be very relativistic
about formulae, saying that this one is as good as another
one. They were all made in good faith, so today we'll

operate off this formula, tomorrow we'll run the same line using a different formula. Well, it doesn't quite work out that way, does it? I certainly don't want a doctor operating on me who would say, "Well, you know, Aristotle's anatomy was performed in good faith and so let's operate and use Aristotle's anatomy today." We do claim that there is a truth status to Christian claims, but that again . . . . Yes, O.K.

P. I was just going to say that I don't think you prove Christianity to anybody by facts. You don't prove Christianity, you don't make converts of people by arguing. You don't make Christians of people by establishing the truth of the gospel, because, in effect, I believe that the truth lies in the spiritual realm. You can call that emotionalism, or what you want to, or anything, but I think the truth lies there. They know about the truth because they have felt it, and if they haven't felt it, they're going to doubt it. I would like to extend that one step further: The discrepancy between the gospels is sufficient to throw great doubt into many people, unless they have felt it.

E. Mr. ——— is saying that in the final analysis no one is brought to Christianity by intellectual argument, they are brought there only by a feeling, a conviction, that Christianity is true, and he says that the discrepancies in the gospels raise a kind of question that intellectual argument alone would not be able to get over. That some feeling of faith has to solve this hurdle. Does that mean that we are not under some obligation to try to understand intellectually the discrepancies?

P. No, I think we are also perhaps intellectually responsible to understand pretty many other things, too. We are probably intellectually responsible to understand, as you would say, the atheism of communism, or the kind of religion of our ancestors way back. I mean, we have an intellectual responsibility; where does it begin and where does it end? I suppose we have an intellectual responsibility to try to understand everything that's within our capacity to understand.

E. All right. . . . We have a comment over here.

P. [This comment was made by a young woman with a soft voice who was a long way from the microphone and is undecipherable. No expletives, however, were deleted.]

E. You are saying that all religions point toward the same God. Just as a matter of specific hard data, just keeping our information straight, there are only three religions in the world that believe in anything we could call a God: Christianity, Judaism, and Islam. The Buddhists, Confucianists, and all of these other people don't believe in anything that would be recognizable to us as a God. Also we would have to deal with the fact that, at least for a number of centuries, it was a part of the Moslem faith that their religion should be spread by the sword, and the way that Islam conquered the Near East as rapidly as it did was by warfare. Now, I think there was more to it than that. People would never have accepted it even at sword's point if they didn't find something more to it than that. Or, if they weren't dissatisfied with what they had previously, or something like that. But when we go from the militarism of Islam to the cult of Shiva and some of the more exotic Hindu and Buddhist cults where torture, all kinds of very nasty things are practiced in the name of religion, I wonder how much we want to say that they are all testimonies to the same thing.

P. Haven't these been done in the name of Christianity?

E. These things have been done in the name of Christianity, but at least in Christianity you could always point to the charter documents and say that anybody who made that claim was speaking in direct contradiction of what Jesus himself said and what the main line of Christian tradition has always been.

P. Christianity is based on the Old Testament. Before Jesus, God used warfare as one of the greatest things to get people on his side. We have to accept the Old Testament as Christian. Therefore, we use warfare, if you want to go by faith. I think the whole thing sets more on: People have to receive the Holy Spirit. The Spirit comes in phases, just like education. You walk up a ladder. I think that at first the other disciples perhaps were a little higher on the ladder with the Spirit and could accept—their faith was strong enough to accept—the empty tomb. Simon Peter and Thomas didn't have the Holy Spirit to the extent the others did, perhaps, and they couldn't accept it until they felt or saw something with their own eyes.

E. So, no one can receive religious truth until he has the Holy Spirit. And the question that raises is: How do you know when what you have is the Holy Spirit? Because the New Testament certainly tells us to test spirits to see whether they are from God or not. And so this too is often not the criterion. (Bell rings.) Well, we didn't get near far enough.

Notes

PART I METHOD

CHAPTER 1

1 R. Bultmann et al., *Kerygma and Myth* (New York: Harper and Row, 1961), p. 5.
2 James Barr, *The Bible in the Modern World* (New York: Harper and Row, 1973), p. 118.
3 Ibid., p. 119.
4 Peter Berger and Thomas Luckmann, *The Social Construction of Reality* (Garden City, New York: Doubleday, 1966).
5 Barr, op. cit., p. 141.
6 Robert S. Ellwood, Jr., *One Way: The Jesus Movement and Its Meaning* (Englewood Cliffs, New Jersey: Prentice-Hall, 1973), p. 31.
7 Willi Marxsen, *Introduction to the New Testament* (Philadelphia: Fortress, 1968), p. 10.

CHAPTER 2

1 Gerhard Ebeling, "Word of God and Hermeneutic," in James M. Robinson and John B. Cobb, eds., *The New Hermeneutic* (New York: Harper and Row, 1964), p. 105.
2 Manfred Mezger, "Preparation for Preaching—The Route from Exegesis to Proclamation," in R. Bultmann et al., *Translating Theology into the Modern Age* (New York: Harper and Row, 1965), p. 165.
3 Ebeling, op. cit., p. 107.
4 Mezger, op. cit., p. 166.
5 Paul Tillich, *Systematic Theology* (Chicago: University of Chicago Press, 1951), vol. I, pp. 64 ff.
6 Ibid., p. 62.

7 Ibid., p. 63.
8 D. Mackenzie Brown, ed., *Ultimate Concern: Tillich in Dialogue* (New York: Harper and Row, 1965), p. 40.
9 Nathan A. Scott, Jr., *Modern Literature and the Religious Frontier* (New York: Harper and Row, 1958), p. x.

<h3 align="center">Chapter 3</h3>

1 A. A. Milne, *Winnie-the-Pooh* (New York: E. P. Dutton, 1926), p. 2.
2 Harry Emerson Fosdick, "What Is the Matter with Preaching?" *Harper's Magazine*, July, 1928.
3 Halford E. Luccock, *In the Minister's Workshop* (Nashville: Abingdon, 1944), p. 56.
4 Clement W. Welsh, *Preaching in a New Key* (Philadelphia: Pilgrim, 1974).
5 Ibid., p. 108.
6 Ibid.
7 Ibid., p. 109.
8 E. Linnemann, *Jesus of the Parables* (New York: Harper and Row, 1967), p. 26.
9 Welsh, op. cit., 109.
10 Clement W. Welsh, *College of Preachers Newsletter*, vol. XX, no. 2 (Spring, 1974), p. 1.

<h2 align="center">PART II   EXAMPLES</h2>

<h3 align="center">Example 1</h3>

1 Günther Bornkamm, "The Stilling of the Storm in Matthew," in Günther Bornkamm, Gerhard Barth, and Heinz Joachim Held, *Tradition and Interpretation in Matthew* (Philadelphia: Westminster, 1963), pp. 52–57.
2 Quentin Quesnell, "Theological Method on the Scripture as Source" in *Foundations of Theology: Papers from the International Lonergan Congress 1970*, ed. Philip McShane (Dublin: Gill and Macmillan, 1971), pp. 189–90.

<h3 align="center">Example 5</h3>

1 Joachim Jeremias, *The Parables of Jesus* (New York: Scribner's, 1963), pp. 65 ff.

<h3 align="center">Example 6</h3>

1 *Christianity Today*, February 25, 1971, p. 30.

2 Frederick C. Grant, *Roman Hellenism and the New Testament* (New York: Scribner's, 1962), p. 171.

EXAMPLE 8

1 *Psychology Today.* November, 1973, p. 89.
2 Ibid.
3 Ibid.

EXAMPLE 9

1 John McKenzie, "Biblical Anthropomorphism and the Humaneness of God," in James M. Robinson, ed., *Religion and the Humanizing of Man* (Waterloo, Ont.: Council on the Study of Religion, 1973), p. 176.
2 Ibid., p. 180.

EXAMPLE 11

1 Flavius Josephus, *Antiquities,* XVIII. v. 2.

EXAMPLE 12

1 Robert N. Bellah, "The Quest For Direction," in Myron B. Bloy, Jr., ed., *Search for the Sacred: The New Spiritual Quest* (New York: Seabury, 1972), p. 77.
2 Yoram Matmor, *Who Me?* (New York: Pocket Books, 1971), p. 107.

EXAMPLE 13

1 Joe R. Feagin, *Psychology Today,* November, 1972.
2 Bob Rowland, *Listen, Christian* (Dayton: Geo. A. Pflaum, 1968).

EXAMPLE 14

1 Welsh, *Preaching in a New Key,* p. 112.
2 "The Year of the Famine," *Newsweek,* June 4, 1973, pp. 44–46.
3 Milton Mayer, *If Men Were Angels* (New York: Atheneum, 1972).
4 Jennie Moore, *The People on Second Street* (New York: Morrow, 1968), pp. 214–215.

EXAMPLE 15

1 C. S. Lewis, *The Screwtape Letters* (New York: Macmillan, 1974), pp. 15 ff.

Helpful Books

An Archbishop of Canterbury is credited with saying that when he visited a clergyman, he liked to look at his books and discover the year in which he died. Many clerical libraries do appear to indicate that their owners are under the impression that biblical scholarship ceased the year they graduated from seminary. Exegesis of the sort described in Chapter One, however, presupposes that one has kept up. What follows is a convenient checklist of current books that will be useful tools for performing the various steps discussed above in hearing what the biblical writer is saying.

TEXTUAL CRITICISM

Bruce M. Metzger, *A Textual Commentary on the Greek New Testament*. London/New York: United Bible Societies, 1971. The United Bible Societies have produced an edition of the Greek New Testament in which significant textual variants are assigned a relative degree of probability (A,B,C, or D). This commentary discusses the reasoning behind those assignments. It is easily consulted since it is arranged in the sequence of New Testament books, chapters, and verses.

BIBLE DICTIONARIES

Interpreter's Dictionary of the Bible, ed. George Buttrick *et al.* New York/Nashville: Abingdon, 1962, 4 vols. One of the most useful sets of reference books a minister can own.

John L. McKenzie, *Dictionary of the Bible*. Milwaukee: Bruce, 1965. The work of one of the most distinguished Roman Catholic biblical scholars in America, this one-volume dictionary is both the triumph of one man's erudition and, in its inexpensive paperbound edition, one of the handiest aids a student can have.

THEOLOGICAL DICTIONARIES OF THE BIBLE

Theological Dictionary of the New Testament, ed. G. Kittel and G. Friederich, trans. G. W. Bromiley. Grand Rapids: Eerdmans, 1964–74, 9 vols. One of the monuments of twentieth-century biblical scholarship, but probably too expensive for the average clergyman's library.

A Theological Word Book of the Bible, ed. Alan Richardson. New York: Macmillan, 1951. A handy, one-volume paperback that is still extremely useful even though a bit dated.

Rudolf Bultmann, *The Theology of the New Testament*, trans. Kendrick Grobel. New York, Scribner's, 1951–55, 2 vols. Not a dictionary, but to my mind still the most reliable guide to the thought of the New Testament writers, although it is definitely obsolete on the thought of the synoptic evangelists. Later works of the same sort worth consulting are those of Conzelmann, Jeremias, and Kümmel.

INTRODUCTIONS TO THE NEW TESTAMENT

Norman Perrin, *The New Testament, An Introduction*. New York/Chicago/San Francisco/Atlanta: Harcourt Brace Jovanovich, 1974. This book is recommended not only as a reference book but also as the best means for anyone who is not absolutely current in New Testament study to catch up on the very latest trends in the field. A similar service may be performed in a more technical way by a book that is not an introduction as such,

James M. Robinson and Helmut Koester, *Trajectories through Early Christianity*. Philadelphia: Fortress Press, 1971. Two introductions that are slightly older than Perrin's that are still quite good are: R. H. Fuller, *A Critical Introduction to the New Testament*. London: Duckworth, 1966; and W. Marxsen, *Introduction to the New Testament*, trans. G. Buswell. Philadelphia: Fortress, 1968.

SYNOPSIS

Synopsis of the Four Gospels, ed. Kurt Aland. London/New York: United Bible Societies, 1972. Publishes the United Bible Societies Greek text on facing pages with the R.S.V. English text. A synopsis with just the English text of the four gospels has been edited by Sparkes, while Huck's old synopsis of just the synoptics has its English counterpart in Burton K. Throckmorton's *Gospel Parallels*.

FORM CRITICISM

Rudolf Bultmann, *The History of the Synoptic Tradition*, trans. John Marsh. Oxford: Blackwell, 1963. The great classic work.

Edgar V. McKnight, *What Is Form Criticism?*, "Guides to Biblical Scholarship." Philadelphia: Fortress, 1969. A good popular introduction to the subject.

REDACTION CRITICISM

Joachim Rohde, *Rediscovering the Teaching of the Evangelists*, trans. D. M. Barton, "New Testament Library." London: SCM, 1968. A history of the discipline of redaction criticism up to the time of writing, this work reports a discouraging variety of interpretations of the evangelists.

Norman Perrin, *What Is Redaction Criticism?*, "Guides to Biblical Scholarship." Philadelphia: Fortress, 1969. A good popular introduction to the discipline by one of the most accomplished practitioners of the method in its American school.

Willi Marxsen, *Mark the Evangelist*, trans. R. A. Harrisville. Nashville/New York: Abingdon, 1969. The pioneer redaction critical study of Mark by the man who coined the name of the technique.

Theodore J. Weeden, *Mark: Traditions in Conflict*. Philadelphia: Fortress, 1971. An example of more recent American work.

Günther Bornkamm, Gerhard Barth, and Heinz Joachim Held, *Tradition and Interpretation in Matthew*, trans. Percy Scott, "New Testament Library." Philadelphia: Westminster, 1963. The initial redaction criticism of Matthew done by one of Germany's leading scholars and two of his pupils.

Hans Conzelmann, *The Theology of St. Luke*, trans. G. Buswell. New York: Harper, 1960. The ground-breaking study of Luke-Acts.

COMMENTARIES

ONE-VOLUME

Interpreter's One-Volume Commentary on the Bible, ed. Charles M. Laymon. Nashville/New York: Abingdon, 1971. This and the fine Roman Catholic work listed next often incorporate more up-to-date scholarship than is available in any full-length commentaries on single books of the Bible.

The Jerome Biblical Commentary, ed. Raymond Brown, Joseph Fitzmyer, and Roland Murphy. Englewood Cliffs, N.J.: Prentice-Hall, 1968.

SERIES

Traditionally scholars have warned clergy against buying series of commentaries because the volumes are usually of a mixed quality, but it appears that the new series being published by Fortress called *Hermeneia* is reliable in its entirety. The commentaries on the New Testament that have appeared so far are:

Colossians and Philemon by Eduard Lohse

The Pastoral Epistles by Martin Dibelius and Hans Conzelmann

The Johannine Epistles by Rudolf Bultmann.

INDIVIDUAL-VOLUME

D. E. Nineham, *The Gospel of St. Mark*, "The Pelican Gospel Commentaries." New York: Seabury, 1968. A student of R. H. Lightfoot, who was doing redaction criticism before it had a name, this accomplished English scholar has written a fine commentary at a quite popular level.

Eduard Schweizer, *The Good News According to Mark*, trans. D. H. Madvig. Richmond: John Knox, 1970. One of the most helpful commentaries for a preacher that I have ever seen since it not only exegetes passages but also comments on their significance.

I have not read any good commentaries in English on Matthew and Luke, but I think it likely that two I have not been able to obtain yet will be a great improvement on anything currently available, those by David Hill and E. Earle Ellis in the "New Century Bible" series currently being published by Oliphants in London.

For the Fourth Gospel there is an embarrassment of riches:

Rudolf Bultmann, *The Gospel of John: A Commentary*, trans. G. R. Beasley-Murray et al. Philadelphia: Westminster, 1971. Although Bultmann's theories about sources, disarrangement, and Gnostic influence have not received universal agreement, he can lead us into the dynamic of the evangelist's thought in a way that few others can.

C. H. Dodd, *The Interpretation of the Fourth Gospel.* Cambridge: Cambridge Univ. Press, 1965. Not a commentary, but a study of the possible backgrounds against which the gospel is to be understood, its key words and leading ideas, and its argument and structure. This last section has the effect of being a short commentary that gives great insight into the relation of a passage to those around it, which, in turn, helps us to see the point the writer is driving at.

Raymond E. Brown, *The Gospel According to John*, "The Anchor Bible." Garden City, N.Y.: Doubleday, 1966–1970, 2 vols. Exhaustive and exhausting, this commentary answers any question anyone might ever have about the Fourth Gospel. It takes the critical insights of Bultmann, tames them down, and gives the most balanced interpretation of this gospel with which I am familiar.

Barnabas Lindars, *The Gospel of John*, "New Century Bible." London: Oliphants, 1972. A very sane and helpful work by a most erudite friar of the Anglican Franciscan order.

Ernst Haenchen, *The Acts of the Apostles: A Commentary*, trans. R. McL. Wilson et al. Philadelphia: Westminster, 1971. Using techniques similar to those of Conzelmann that he developed independently, Haenchen has written here what I consider to be the most satisfactory commentary on a biblical book that I have ever read.

MISCELLANEOUS

Joachim Jeremias, *The Parables of Jesus*, trans. S. H. Hooke. London: SCM, 1954. I tell my students at the seminary that they have no moral right to preach on a parable until they have read what Jeremias has to say about it.

EXEGETICAL AIDS FOR PREACHING

Although I do not think that the use of someone else's exegetical notes is ever an acceptable alternative to doing one's own homework, there are two series to which attention ought to be called. In its *Proclamation* series, Fortress Press has twenty-four short books, one for each of the eight annual liturgical seasons in the three-year lectionary cycle of most major denominations, which contain about a printed page on each of the lessons appointed for that season written by a biblical scholar, and another page on each written by someone qualified to give suggestions for homiletical development of the exegesis. Another such service is the commentary on the epistles and gospels that *Worship* magazine has commissioned R. H. Fuller to do, and which has recently appeared in a convenient single volume under the title, *Preaching the New Lectionary: The Word of God for the Church Today*. Collegeville, Minn.: The Liturgical Press, 1975. Users of either service may be confident that they are being guided by sound scholarship.